THE CIVILIZATION OF THE AMERICAN INDIAN SERIES

# THE WORLD OF THE CROW INDIANS

# THE WORLD OF
# THE CROW INDIANS

## As Driftwood Lodges

by Rodney Frey

UNIVERSITY OF OKLAHOMA PRESS : NORMAN AND LONDON

E
99
C92
F74
1993

**Library of Congress Cataloging-in-Publication Data**

Frey, Rodney, 1950–
  The world of the Crow Indian.

  (The Civilization of the American Indian series;
v. 185)
  Bibliography: p. 185.
  Includes index.
  1. Crow Indians—Philosophy.   2. Crow Indians—
Religion and mythology.   3. Indians of North America—
Montana—Philosophy.   4. Indians of North America—
Montana—Religion and mythology.   I. Title.   II. Series.
E99.C92F74   1987      306'.4      87-40212
ISBN: 0–8061–2076–2 (cloth)
ISBN: 0–8061–2560–8 (paper)

*The World of the Crow Indians: As Driftwood Lodges* is Volume
185 in The Civilization of the American Indian Series.

The paper in this book meets the guidelines for permanence and
durability of the Committee on Production Guidelines for Book
Longevity of the Council on Library Resources, Inc. ∞

4   5   6   7   8   9   10   11   12

To Matthew
and all the other sons and daughters
who need to know and remember

and to Tom and Susie
and all the other grandparents
who have helped us to know and remember

# Contents

# Illustrations

# Maps

# Preface

ON A HOT JULY AFTERNOON an old Apsáalooke man and I sat on a bench in the shade of a huge cottonwood tree. He was an "announcer," experienced in his culture, articulate in his explanation of it, and patient with the often naïve and shortsighted questions I was asking him. Families and clan uncles, politics and tribal councils, and religion and sweat baths were among the diverse topics on which I sought his comment. About an hour into the quizzing and perhaps growing less patient, the old man stopped me. Pointing to a highway department building some fifty yards to the north, he said,

You see that tin shed? It's like my culture. You can sit back here, ask questions, and describe it. But it's not 'til you get inside, 'til you see what's inside and feel it, that you *really know* what the tin shed is about. You can't stand outside; you've got to go inside.

We took a walk, and I was led into the tin shed.

This book attempts to share something of what is inside the tin shed, describing the world as viewed by the Apsáalooke (Crow Indians).

In accord with Åke Hultkrantz's call for "continued field investigation" into "traditional religions" (1976:90–91), this material is the result of an association with the Apsáalooke people of the Crow Indian Reservation in Montana. The association began in June, 1974, and it continues today. From 1974 through 1979, I resided much of the time on the reservation, learning the language of the Apsáalooke (though I remain far from fluent), living with an Apsáalooke family, and participating fully in the varied dimensions of their lives. This involvement led me to the Sun Dance. The Sun Dance ceremony has been particularly important to me personally. Each summer since 1974 I have assisted in the ceremony by helping erect the lodge and gather the ritual items needed by the dancers. On six occasions I have "used the whistle" as a participant. A few days before "going in" the 1977 Sun Dance, Tom Yellowtail gave me a gift I have cherished. During the opening of a medicine bundle, he bestowed on me the name Maakuuxshiichíilish, meaning "seeking to help others." I hope that this book contributes to the responsibility that was bestowed upon me with that name.

My concern here is with the contemporary nature of the Apsáalooke. Thus I incorporate only minimally the existing scholarly literature. Most of that literature focuses on the cultural and religious orientation of the Apsáalooke in the buffalo days rather than on their contemporary culture. Two important exceptions are Michael Fitzgerald's forthcoming *Yellowtail* (tentative title) and Fred Voget's *Shoshoni-Crow Sun Dance*. Additional pertinent works on the Apsáalooke are listed in the bibliography. An earlier version of this book appeared as my Ph.D. dissertation, "To Dance Together: Ethnography in Apsáalooke (Crow) Culture" (University of Colorado, 1979).

Robert Lowie, the premier ethnographer of the Apsáalooke, did his primary research between 1907 and 1916. At that time he was employed by the American Museum of Natural History, under the direction of Clark Wissler. As with much ethnographic research of that period, Lowie's was conducted as "salvage ethnography." Anthropologists expected that the indigenous tribal peoples would soon vanish, and thus they perceived an urgent need to record their ways of life. Although Lowie's contribution to Apsáalooke ethnography is irrefutably significant (his 1935 book, *The Crow Indians*, is, in fact, a classic), gaps remain, and additions are needed. There is an "irritating barrenness" in the description of religion and ritual symbolism (Hult-krantz 1976:90). Despite Lowie's devotion of the final chapter of *The Crow Indians* to world view, his treatment of the subject is brief and focuses entirely on a view indicative of the buffalo days. No other attempts have been made since Lowie's to describe the Apsáalooke world view. Given that the Apsáalooke have not vanished, and are far from doing so, the need for additional comment is particularly keen. Many of their institutions continue virtually unchanged at present from their status seventy years ago, when Lowie conducted his primary research. *The World of the Crow Indians* thus contributes to an understanding of, but by no means makes a definitive statement on, Apsáalooke world view and describes two institutions, *áassahke* (clan uncle and aunt) and *xapáaliia* (medicine), that have resisted the tremendous pressures of Euro-American assimilation.

My intent is to describe rather than to analyze the Apsáalooke world view. It is significant that certain institutions have resisted Euro-American pressures of assimilation, while others have been drastically altered, either vanishing altogether or becoming integrated into the larger reservation and societal structures. Such issues are timely and certainly merit further consideration. Such analysis, however, lies outside the scope of this book. Voget's solid ethnographic research has made a significant contribution to such study by placing the Apsáalooke, and especially the Sun Dance, in their historical and cultural contexts. Voget's *Shoshoni-Crow Sun Dance*, with its emphasis on the acculturation processes affecting the Apsáalooke, is therefore a fine complement to this book.

My goal is to present the ethnographic materials from the perspective of the Apsáalooke, reflecting the view from the interior of the tin shed. This world view involves an immense clan and kin network, participated in by the Buffalo and the Little People; the Sun Dance, with its sacrificial offerings, journeys to other worlds, and healings by medicine men; and an oral literature rich in heroes and tricksters. It is a view of hope and strength that has served the

Apsáalooke well. My descriptions of ceremonies and situations and their meanings may at times seem surrealistic as well as idealistic or even prescriptive. This is a function of the manner in which the Apsáalooke see themselves and their world. After all, what I describe is as much a particular *view* of what occurs as it is what occurs. In the world of the Apsáalooke, the Little People can reveal themselves, Eagles can communicate, the Feathers of a medicine man can heal, and spoken words can create.

To convey a sense of the texture and tone of the Apsáalooke world, I have included drawings, photographs, and short narratives. I drew the illustrations and took the photographs especially for this book. They reflect sights commonly associated with the Apsáalooke landscape. Important to that landscape are numerous local and reservationwide powwows involving dancers adorned in finely beaded garments. I have included as ornaments throughout the book designs based on Apsáalooke beading patterns. The narratives characterize events as they are experienced and shared among the Apsáalooke. They are based on my own participation and observations and on accounts related to me by informants. With only a few exceptions, all of the situations referred to in the narratives occurred within the past twenty years. A few of the narratives are taken from the oral literature of the Apsáalooke, stories from the buffalo days still told today. These stories introduce many Apsáalooke culture heroes, including Old Man Coyote, Burnt Face, and the brothers Curtain Boy and Spring Boy. While I have not attempted to replicate the idiom of Apsáalooke storytelling, I have tried to present each narrative in a manner that is easily identifiable to the Apsáalooke. To ensure this, I retold each account to my informants, and they, in turn, clarified and corrected them when necessary. During the writing of this book, I maintained a close dialogue with, and elicited response from, virtually everyone who helped bring the Apsáalooke world alive in these pages.

While almost all the Apsáalooke are bilingual, their

native language predominates in virtually all family and ceremonial situations. Because many terms are not easily translated into English, and because I have attempted to demonstrate the Apsáalooke perspective, I have given preference to Apsáalooke terms over their English counterparts. Frequently heard Apsáalooke expressions are incorporated into the text to help delineate the contours and boundaries of the Apsáalooke world. In addition, English phrases frequently used by the Apsáalooke are also incorporated, appearing in quotation marks. A glossary and a pronunciation key are included at the end of the book.

Having stated my *intent*—to describe the contemporary world as viewed by Apsáalooke men and women—I must also acknowledge that as a male Euro-American, raised in a tradition alien to that of the Apsáalooke, I must necessarily fall short of my goal. Although I have entered the tin shed and endeavored to be attentive and sensitive to the full range of Apsáalooke experience and thought, many areas of the tin shed never were and never could be explored. While I have learned something of the Apsáalooke language and have begun to comprehend and speak it, I have never conceptualized or dreamed as an Apsáalooke. While I have interviewed and observed Apsáalooke women in a variety of settings, much of their experience remains veiled to me. While I have heard stories of people and events of twenty years ago, or even of the buffalo days, I did not experience those days as a child, and I will never look back upon them as an elder.

The interior of the Apsáalooke tin shed is a great labyrinth. Others, including the Apsáalooke themselves, must complete the portrait and reveal the full depth of meaning and beauty that is the Apsáalooke world view.

RODNEY FREY

*Helena, Montana*

# Acknowledgments

I WISH TO GIVE THANKS to all the Apsáalooke people, especially to the Old Coyote, Old Horn, and Real Bird families, who opened their lives to me in so many ways, and to John Trehero, who guided me in times of need and whose stories brought the Apsáalooke culture to life. I am also particularly grateful to the Yellowtail family, especially Tom and Susie, who took me in as a grandson, shared their lives with me, and allowed me to grow. Without their help this book could not have been written. "Ahóo."

I would also like to thank Father Randolph Graczyk, of the Saint Charles Mission, Pryor, Montana, who with deep sensitivity and respect introduced me to the Sun Dance religion, offered invaluable suggestions on this book, and assisted me in assembling the Apsáalooke glossary. "Ahóo."

Among others who have been instrumental in the development of this book are Nancy Breuninger and Cheryl McCauley, of Helena, Montana, who patiently retyped its many drafts; Joseph Epes Brown, Department of Religious Studies, University of Montana, whose life-style and writings represent the finest example available of the Indian spirit translated for the non-Indian; David Carrasco, Department of Religious Studies, University of Colorado, whose enthusiasm inspired me and who introduced me to the writings of Mircea Eliade, which allowed me to better appreciate the Apsáalooke world; Rose and Steve Chesarech, Crow Bilingual Education, who patiently taught me the Apsáalooke language and shared the Apsáalooke culture with me; C. Adrian Heidenreich, Department of Native American Studies, Eastern Montana College, who shared with me his numerous insights into Apsáalooke history and made valuable bibliographic suggestions; Åke Hultkrantz, Institute of Comparative Religion, University of Stockholm, who set high academic standards for me to emulate; G. Hubert Matthews, Crow Bilingual Education, who introduced me to the complexities of Apsáalooke language; Chris McGonigle, of Helena, and Patty Dornbusch, of the University of Oklahoma Press, who gave me invaluable editing and writing lessons; Joe Medicine Crow, the Crow Tribal Historian, who warmly shared his knowledge of history and culture; Sally Old Coyote, Crow Bilingual Education, who shared with me her 1971 Sun Dance photographs, which inspired three of the drawings in this book; Jack Schultz, Department of Anthropology, Colorado State University, who introduced me to the Apsáalooke; Deward Walker, Department of Anthropology, University of Colorado, who encouraged my intellectual growth in Apsáalooke culture; Sister Karen Watembach, Crow Catholic Religion Research Center, who gave me the opportunity to do fieldwork on Apsáalooke social organization; and the photographer whose name I never learned (for which I apologize), who shared with me his wonderful images of the 1974 Sun Dance, which inspired four of the drawings in this book. "Ahóo."

For their encouragement and continued support, a special thanks to my family. "Ahóo."

For permission to reprint excerpts from copyrighted materials, I am indebted to the following:

University of Chicago Press, Chicago: Fred Eggan, ed. *Social Organization of the North American Indian Tribes*, 1955; Alfonso Ortiz, *The Tewa World: Space, Time, Being, and Becoming in a Pueblo Society*, 1969.
Dover, New York: George Catlin, *Letters and Notes on the Manners, Customs and Conditions of the North American Indians*, 1973.

Harper & Row, New York: Åke Hultkrantz, "The Contribution of
    the Study of North American Indian Religions to the History
    of Religions." In *Seeing with the Native Eye: Contributions
    to the Study of Native American Religion*, edited by Walter
    H. Capps, 1976; Frank Linderman, *Plenty-coups, Chief of
    the Crows*, 1930.
Holt, Rinehart and Winston, New York: Robert Lowie, *The Crow
    Indians*, 1935.
Indian Historian Press, San Francisco: N. Scott Momaday, "Man
    Made of Words." In *Indian Voices: The First Convocation of
    American Indian Scholars*, edited by Rupert Costo, 1970.

                                                      R. F.

# THE WORLD OF THE CROW INDIANS

# CHAPTER 1

# As Driftwood Lodges (*Ashammaléaxia*): A World View

THE APSÁALOOKE have always lived in close association with the land, its animals, its plants, and its seasonal cycles. They know the buffalo, the chokecherry, and the river as they know their own children. And through this kinship, they have been receptive to any lessons the buffalo or the river have had to offer.

As one gazes out upon the Yellowstone or the Bighorn River, especially during the heavy spring runoff, it is not uncommon to see driftwood floating down the river. Often the driftwood vanishes from view, submerged in an eddy or smashed against a boulder. But also clearly visible is the driftwood that survives, woven together in a bundle along the riverbanks. A lesson is offered.

The Apsáalooke term for clan is *ashammaléaxia*, which translates "as driftwood lodges."[1] As driftwood lodges together along the banks of the rivers, so the members of a clan cling together, united in a turbulent stream. Each individual is like a piece of driftwood, orienting himself or herself around, and depending on, the others of the prescribed group. The driftwood bundle must remain tightly bound, for the river's fast currents and protruding boulders would smash and submerge an isolated piece of driftwood. An individual would find it exceedingly difficult to float alone, confronting adversaries at every bend. To maintain the

---

[1] See the glossary at the end of this book for definitions and pronunciations of Apsáalooke words and phrases.

Driftwood along the bank of the Little Bighorn River, near Wyola, Montana.

group's integrity and his or her membership within it, each individual participates in gift exchanges with others; each gives to the others, and in return the driftwood lodges.

The metaphor of the driftwood lodging is not limited to the Apsáalooke clan structure. It has a broader application. In fact, it is ingrained in much of the Apsáalooke world view.[2]

The Apsáalooke view a world in which all entities and all phenomena are interconnected, animal with plant with land with human with spirit. The human being is intrinsically linked to and part of the assemblage of human and spiritual personages that surrounds him or her. The world and the individual are necessarily not separate and autonomous. The focus of the individual's identity and activities is

[2] See the Appendix for a discussion of the concept of world view.

not on the self as a self-reliant entity but rather on the network of human and spiritual beings of which he or she is a part. The world does not exist in a void, meaningless and inanimate, but rather it has a dynamics and a vitality upon which all entities interdepend. It is animated with meaningful patterns and a life-force. A human being does not so much assert control over the world as attend to the guidance and transformative power offered in it. In exchange for what is offered, and to maintain participation in this world, the individual reciprocates unselfishly. Gift exchange characterizes human and spiritual relationships. Consequently the individual's immediate world is neither one of abandonment nor one inhabited by adversaries. It is a home to human and spiritual kinfolk, and it is endowed with significance and life. While participating in this world, a human being is assured of support, adopted by that which is greater than the self. The driftwood lodges together.

While the material world is certainly acknowledged and never denied in the pragmatism of the Apsáalooke, the levels of transcendence from the material world are invested with a more meaningful reality. The phenomenal world understood and entered into by the Apsáalooke includes the transcendent world.[3] For one to comprehend "Indian medicine," for example, one must appreciate the level of reality on which it transpires and affects the lives of the Apsáalooke. To attempt to comprehend it solely on a material plane is to misinterpret its meaning and significance, which the Apsáalooke derive from the transcendent plane. What the Apsáalooke refer to as the "spiritual" is equivalent to the transcendent. Both terms are used interchangeably in this book.

The salient qualities of the Apsáalooke world view involve an image of the world in which all entities (human, natural, and spiritual) are unified and interconnected; the

---

[3]This view is not unlike Plato's allegory of the cave, with its levels of reality in which the transcendent forms are absolute, while the material world is merely a transitory reflection of them (*Republic*, book 7).

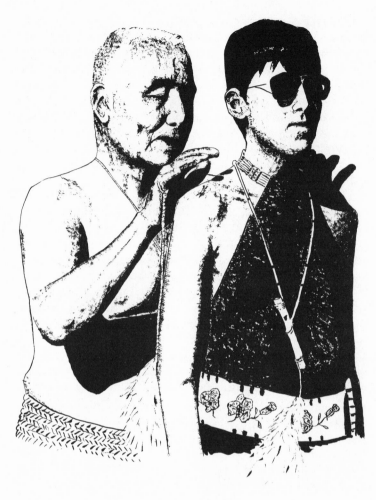

A Sun Dancer receives a prayer from his clan uncle, Tom Yellowtail, at the close of the Ashkísshe.

relationships among these entities are characterized by reciprocity; the world is animated and permeated with meaning and life-force; and the phenomenal world includes the transcendent. To illustrate these qualities, the institutions of *áassahke* (the clan uncle and aunt relation) and *xapáaliia* (medicine) and a metaphor, the "wagon wheel," are considered. The wagon wheel, besides illustrating the four world-view qualities, also suggests the manner in which the Apsáalooke express and mediate two perennial existential dilemmas: differentiation versus oneness and receptivity and dependence versus creativity and volition.

The wagon wheel, *xapáaliia,* and *áassahke* are discussed in this book not to reveal the detail and full extent of each but to illustrate a world view. These are not the only examples that could be used. The "driftwood" world view can also be found clearly expressed in the activities of the Native American Church (the Peyote religion) or the Apsáalooke understanding of the Roman Catholic church and in all dimensions of Apsáalooke family and clan life. In Fitzgerald's vivid life history (forthcoming) of Tom Yellowtail, the man and his deeds personify the meaning of "as driftwood lodges." Tom Yellowtail is also prominent among the many Apsáalooke who have contributed their stories and understandings to this book.

# CHAPTER 2

# Historical Sketch of the Apsáalooke

THE HISTORY OF THE APSÁALOOKE reveals the antiquity and tenacity of the "driftwood" world view.[1] Apsáalooke oral history begins with Isáahkawuattee, Old Man Coyote. While most of his adventures or, more appropriately, misadventures reflect the trickster character par excellence, he is also acknowledged as the creator of the world and of all that is primary in Apsáalooke society.

## The Journey

In the mid-sixteenth century, the ancestral tribe of the present-day Hidatsa and Apsáalooke lived in a land known as the "tree country" or "land of the lakes," the Winnipeg country of southeastern Manitoba. Not only historically related, the Hidatsa and the Apsáalooke also share a close linguistic affinity. Both languages are Siouan, and many Apsáalooke maintain that, with a little patience, both are still mutually understandable. Prompted either by pressures from hostile tribes moving into their territory or by the lure of better lands for hunting and farming, the tribe moved to the "Sacred Waters," Devil's Lake, in northeastern North Dakota. A westward migration had begun.

At the "Sacred Waters" two chiefs, No Vitals and Red Scout, fasted and sought spiritual guidance for the tribe's

---

[1] For more detailed accounts of Apsáalooke history see Bradley (1970), Brown (1961), Heidenreich (1985), Marquis (1974), Nabokov (1967), Oswalt (1978), and Voget (1984).

## THE ORIGIN

It's Old Man Coyote. He's traveling about in a world cold and wet, for there's no dry land anywhere. And when he wants to rest, he must lie in the cold and wet waters. Old Man Coyote is having a difficult time of it and is very lonely. Four ducks fly over, and Old Man Coyote asks these younger brothers if they will dive beneath the waters and bring up some earth so that he can make the land. The first duck dives down and attempts to bring up some mud. But when he surfaces, he has no earth. A second, then a third duck dives, but as the first was unsuccessful, so are these. Finally Old Man Coyote asks the fourth duck, Hell-diver, to bring up some earth. Hell-diver stays below the water a long time, so long that Old Man Coyote fears for the duck's life. But when he finally emerges he has a little mud in his webbed feet. With this earth, Old Man Coyote travels to the west, moving with the Sun, and as he does he spreads the mud and makes the land. He places hills, mountains, and coulees as he goes.

After Old Man Coyote makes the land, he places all the animals, grasses, and trees on it and gives them life.

But still the land is a lonely place. So Old Man Coyote rolls and molds from the earth an image he likes and bakes it. Old Man Coyote then blows a small breath into the figure, and it moves. As the man came first, so he shall be first in all things. But not completely satisfied with the image he made, Old Man Coyote tries it again. Woman is then molded and given life. He likes this image a lot better. She is to keep the man's home and cook the food he brings home. Old Man Coyote is no longer alone.

Old Man Coyote teaches the people how to live and pray; he gives them their language; he shows them the Sun Dance; and Old Man Coyote tells them to always remember that they are part of the Earth. The people grow in number and are happy.

While Old Man Coyote is away, at the camp of the people a fight breaks out between two boys. The mothers of the boys come, each defending her own son against the other. Soon the entire land is in an uproar. Everyone is fighting and yelling at each other. It's quite a disturbance. Old Man Coyote returns to camp. He states that from now on the entire camp shall be divided into groups like driftwood that lodges along a river bank and be called "as driftwood lodges." And because it was the

The view west from a point between Lodge Grass and Saint Xavier, Montana.

mothers who defended the boys, the groups shall be made up of the children of the mothers of each group.

The people move on, travelling across the land, occasionally meeting Old Man Coyote.*

*This origin account was shared with me by an informant, and, although shorter, it closely parallels the account recorded by Lowie (1918:14–17).

continued journey. In his dream, Red Scout received a kernel of corn and was instructed to plant the seed, which would provide food for his people. No Vitals received a pod of tobacco seeds and was told to continue the migration into the western mountains, where the seeds should be planted. Not to be smoked, the tobacco was to be harvested only for its seed. When the harvest was bountiful and the tobacco flourished, so too would No Vital's people flourish.

The ancestral Apsáalooke-Hidatsa tribe stayed together during much of its westward migration. Upon meeting the Mandan peoples near the mouth of the Heart River, along the Missouri River in North Dakota, the tribe began pursuing a more sedentary way of life. Living among the Mandan, the tribe built earthen lodges, made pottery, and grew corn, squash, and beans. Supplementing their horticulture, the tribe hunted game animals, such as buffalo and deer.

The exact date of the separation of the Apsáalooke from the Hidatsa is an open question, dependent on various archaeological, linguistic, and oral-history interpretations. Actually, there may have been no exact separation but rather periodic movements of peoples away from, and occasionally back to, the parent group.[2] One such group eventually planted the sacred tobacco seeds near Cloud Peak, in northern Wyoming, several generations after No Vitals' passing. That group, which the Hidatsa called Apsáalooke, meaning "children of the large-beaked bird," finally fulfilled No Vitals' vision. They have remained apart from the Hidatsa ever since.

Joe Medicine Crow, the Crow tribal historian, suggests that the Apsáalooke may have made their final separation from the Hidatsa as early as 1600 to 1624. The linguist G. Hubert Matthews has suggested, on the basis of glottochronology, that the groups have been separated for at least five hundred years, if not longer (1979:113–25). George

[2]See Davis (1979) for an overview of the Apsáalooke-Hidatsa separation from the perspectives of various disciplines.

Frison, an archaeologist, has identified as Apsáalooke northern Wyoming buffalo jump and butchering sites that date
back to the 1500s (1979:3–16). In any event, the Apsáalooke migration onto the northern plains of Wyoming and
Montana preceded the cultural revolution brought about
by the arrival of the horse.

## The Buffalo Days

With the arrival of the horse through Euro-American contact and trade, the Apsáalooke began moving with the buffalo, living in tipis, and abandoning all horticultural pur-
suits except tobacco planting. The harvesting of the sacred
seeds has continued into the present.[3] The Apsáalooke may
have acquired their first horses as early as 1735 through
trade relations that extended to "Indians near the Great
Salt Lake," according to Joe Medicine Crow. The Shoshoni,
who subsequently maintained close ties with the Apsáalooke, were perhaps a critical intermediary in this trade network. For the Apsáalooke, as for other Plains Indians, the
eighteenth century was thus a period of important change
and coalescence, when the cultural patterning that Lowie
has described as "a living culture" was formed (1983:xvii).
It was the era of the buffalo days.[4]

The horse enabled the Apsáalooke to pursue the buffalo
year round. In turn, the buffalo provided meat for food,
bones and horns for tools, dung for cooking fuel, and hides
for clothing, robes, tipi covers, and rawhide containers.
Many of these necessities were provided by other animals
as well—meat, hides, and tools came from elk, deer, and
rabbits. Complementing the meat was a diet rich in various
seasonal berries and roots, such as chokecherries and wild
turnips, and an abundance of corn, beans, and squash obtained in trade with the Hidatsa and the Mandan. But the
buffalo was the focus of subsistence activities.

[3] See Lowie (1983:274–96) for a discussion of the Tobacco Society.
[4] For an analysis of the horse's effect on Plains Indian culture, see Ewers (1955),
and for a description of the buffalo-day Apsáalooke, see Lowie's various accounts,
Linderman (1962 and 1974), Nabokov (1967), and Voget (1984).

The Buffalo, Bishée

Even today, over one hundred years after the passing of the great herds, the buffalo still holds a position of prominence among the Apsáalooke. Although buffalo is no longer part of the daily diet, the tribe maintains a small herd. Occasionally one of the animals is killed and butchered and its meat served at a public gathering, such as the installation of a newly elected tribal official or the feast following a Sun Dance. For the older members of at least one family, few activities provide as much excitement as watching home movies shot of a buffalo hunt over thirty years ago. In the Sun Dance Lodge of today, the mounted head of the Buffalo, hung from the center pole, still nurtures and sustains the Apsáalooke in spirit if not in body. As in the past, the

Buffalo serves as the vision guide for many participants in the Sun Dance.

During the buffalo days ceremonialism among the Apsáalooke was diverse and pervasive. Virtually every dimension of life was inundated with some form of ritual observance. Upon waking, an Apsáalooke might light a pipe and offer a prayer to the morning Sun. One who possessed a medicine bundle would often move it from its place of honor in the lodge and set it outside on a tripod to warm in the Sun. The bundle's contents might have been acquired when a father had fasted for several days alone in the nearby mountains. A vision had come in which an Elk, a Buffalo, or even a Chickadee had given advice and perhaps the spiritual power to effect a cure, locate the buffalo, or capture an Arapaho pony. The bundle was opened on occasions when this power, known as *baaxpée*, was needed. For example, when a horse raid on a Blackfeet camp was to be undertaken, the war shield on which the image of a great Bird was painted and several of its feathers were hung might be taken from the bundle and carried by a warrior. Upon returning with several horses, many of which would be given to kinsmen, the warrior would give credit for his success to the Bird's watchful eye and swift speed. The Bird's qualities had become those of the warrior.

Two examples of the rich diversity of buffalo-day ceremonialism can be found in the sweat bath and the Sun Dance. Perhaps none of the ceremonies is more primal and exemplary than the sweat bath, and perhaps none is more spectacular, and yet transitory and dependent on social circumstances, than the Sun Dance.

Conducted in a small, domed structure made of willow saplings and covered with hide, the sweat bath was a ritual of prayer, offering, and purification. If a crisis arose—for example, the illness of a relative—an individual might pledge to take a sweat as an offering to help the afflicted. On another occasion an individual might have been instructed during a dream to take a sweat. The next day the instruction would be carried out. Before an important un-

## THE FIRST SWEAT BATH

There's a man that becomes a reptile and lives at the bottom of a pond. Because he has very sharp teeth, he's very dangerous. So the people gather together to decide what to do. They come up with an idea. Wearing tough rawhide gloves, they are able to capture the reptile without getting hurt. They then place him in a small, domed-shaped lodge and fill it with hot rocks and water. In the steam and with prayer, he is turned back into a man. When he tries to reenter the pond, he can't sink and only floats. That's how we began the sweat bath. It's good for you.

dertaking—a long journey, a horse raid, or a vision quest—
prayer would be offered in the sweat, and spiritual cleansing and renewal would be attained.

The sweat ritual had four cycles. First, after rocks heated
over an open fire had been placed in a central pit and the
participants had entered, the lodge was sealed, and four
dippers of water were poured over the rocks to fill the
lodge with steam. Prayers and songs were offered. After
the door had been briefly opened to refresh the participants, the second cycle began. This time, seven dippers of
water were poured over the rocks. Again, prayer and song
were offered. In the third cycle, ten dippers of water were
poured, and in the fourth, an uncounted number, again
accompanied by prayer and song. With the completion of
the fourth cycle, the door was opened, and the participants
plunged into a nearby creek or river.

By undergoing the four cycles of the sweat bath, the participants came to recognize its association with the four sea-
sons, the four directions of the circle, and the four components of the world—fire, rock, water, and air (Graczsk
1975). In the sweat ritual, the participants merged their essence with the primal elements, facilitating prayer, sacrifice, and spiritual cleansing.

The Apsáalooke Sun Dance in the buffalo days focused
on gaining power for vengeance (Lowie 1983:297). After the
death of a relative at the hands of an enemy, a man would
sponsor the ritual to gain a vision and spiritual aid to avenge
the killing. The duration of the ceremony depended upon
the length of time necessary for the sponsor to gain what he
sought, usually three days, though sometimes longer. To ar-
range a dance, the sponsor would approach the "owner" of
a Sun Dance doll. The "owner" would coordinate the ceremony and consecrate the event with his Sun Dance doll–
medicine bundle, which was the vehicle through which a
vision could be obtained. As word of the upcoming ceremony spread, others would decide to join the "whistler," as
the sponsor was called, in abstaining from food and water

for the duration of the Sun Dance. They too would be seeking a means to spiritual understanding and power.

Unlike the contemporary Sun Dance, the buffalo-day Sun Dance had only a few participants, all of whom were men and all of whom had themselves pierced and tethered through the breast or shoulders to the lodge structure. Participants attempted to break free as they danced. The "whistler" was an exception. He did not undergo the skin offering. The piercing was a means of sacrifice, of giving a personal gift in exchange for what was sought.

The structure of the Sun Dance Lodge resembled that of a tipi, although it was two to three times larger than the average lodge. In place of hide covers, bundles of willow branches were tied along the poles from top to bottom. A replica of the Sun Dance Lodge was made by one of Lowie's informants, Red-eye (1915:40). The model clearly illustrates the tipi construction of the lodge as well as the placement of the piercing ropes. During each stage of the lodge's erection and use, strict rituals were observed. The lodgepoles were envisioned as an enemy, and when they were cut, coup was struck.

With the "owner's" small buckskin Sun Dance doll tied to the lodge, a group of singers at hand, and the relatives of the participants looking on, the dance would begin. The "whistler" would gaze at the Sun Dance doll and dance continuously until he received a vision. Mock battles would also occur in the lodge, with the Apsáalooke triumphing over their enemies. After the "whistler" received his revelation, cooked buffalo tongues would be given to the participants, and the Sun Dance would end. Only time would tell whether the vision would enable the desired revenge.

As spectacular as the Sun Dance must have been, part of the reason it flourished during the nineteenth century was because the Apsáalooke found themselves in changed circumstances. Although its origins are clouded in obscurity, the Plains Indian–Sun Dance complex probably evolved fully and took on its ceremonial character only after no-

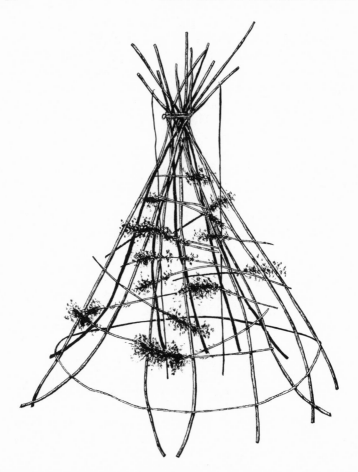

Red-eye's replica of the Sun Dance Lodge (after Lowie 1915:40).

madic peoples, such as the Cheyenne and the Lakota, moved onto the plains and interacted with sedentary peoples, such as the Mandan and the Arikara.[5] In the instance of the Apsáalooke Sun Dance, sponsorship depended on the in-

[5] For a discussion of the diffusion of the Sun Dance among the Plains Indians, see Spier (1921).

tertribal conflict that was encountered after coming onto
the northern plains. Without the conflict, the overt reason
for holding the Sun Dance would not have existed. If the
Apsáalooke Sun Dance had been a ceremony of spiritual renewal and tribal solidarity, as it was for the Cheyenne, it
probably would have been held yearly. But the Apsáalooke
Sun Dance was originally held only every three or four
years, and sometimes less frequently.

As the arrival of the horse brought tremendous changes
to Apsáalooke society, it also brought the Apsáalooke into
direct conflict with a host of formidable adversaries. With
their migration into the region of the Yellowstone River,
the Apsáalooke found themselves neighbors to the Arapaho, the Blackfeet, the Cheyenne, and the Lakota (Sioux),
all of whom claimed, at various times, much of this territory as their own. Both the Blackfeet and the Lakota far
outnumbered the Apsáalooke.

The Apsáalooke were not alone in their struggle. They
maintained alliances, though not always secure, with the
Hidatsa, the Nez Percé, the Salish, and the Shoshoni. In
1805 more than one hundred Shoshoni traveled with the
Apsáalooke for much of the year.

But the Apsáalooke continued to face turbulence. From
1830 to 1870 non-Indian observers consistently predicted
the extermination of the Apsáalooke at the hands of their
adversaries. The artist George Catlin observed in 1832 that
the Apsáalooke "are a much smaller tribe than the Blackfeet, with whom they are always at war, and from whose
great numbers they suffer prodigiously in battle; and probably will be in a few years entirely destroyed by them"
(1973:42–43). In the winter of 1856 the fur trader Edwin
Denig wrote that the Apsáalooke "cannot exist long as a nation, . . . warred against by the Blackfeet on one side and
most bands of the Sioux on the other" (1961:204).

Indeed, the horse raids escalated on occasion to battles
involving hundreds of warriors and extensive loss of life and
property, the women and children of the defeated camp
being kept by the victor. More than any other tribe, the

## ADVERSARIES

A young warrior and a much older man, a medicine man, are out traveling when a large party of Cheyenne spot them and give chase. They make it to a thick, forested creek bed just as the sun is setting. The Cheyenne have them surrounded, but because it's getting dark, they decide to wait 'til morning. Then they'll rush them. Camp fires are set up all 'round the wooded area; there's no chance of escape.

After a while, the old man makes medicine, asking help from his spirit helpers. He also asks the young man, "Do you want to live?" He gets a quick, "Yes!" "Then you must do exactly what I say. Take off all your clothes except your breechcloth and moccasins, and leave all your things over there," pointing to the base of a nearby tree. "Now, close your eyes, never open them 'til I say to and hold tight to my waist."

The two of them begin to move a little. But as they do the young man opens his eyes and they're right where they'd been standing.

"Do you want to live? Then keep your eyes closed!"

They begin to move again, but after awhile the young man gets scared and opens his eyes. They're right where they'd been.

"Do you want to live? Then do as I say!"

So they start off again. The young man really tries to keep them closed, but he knows there's Cheyenne everywhere. Just one quick look. They're standing right where they'd been all along.

"The sun is almost up and the Cheyenne will be in here. Close your eyes if you want to live!"

The young man closes his eyes and holds tight to the old man. He feels light, like a feather.

The sun is up and the Cheyenne rush the wooded creek bed from all sides. But they find nothing. Their own medicine man discovers that the Apsáalooke had made medicine and, in the dark, flew right over them, out of the woods. They find the place where the two men landed. But that's it.

This happened just east of what is now Crow Agency.

Apsáalooke readily adopted Blackfeet and Lakota women and children into their families. The oral history includes a story of one of these battles, which occurred near Pryor, Montana, during the mid-1860s. Several hundred allied Arapaho, Cheyenne, and Lakota warriors attempted to annihilate a large Apsáalooke encampment. Although outnumbered ten to one, the Apsáalooke repulsed the attack.

Despite overwhelming odds the Apsáalooke held fast to an area desired by many. Not only did they hold fast, but they prospered, becoming "perhaps the richest nation in horses of any residing east of the Rocky Mountains" (Denig 1961:144). Families commonly had up to one hundred horses and several well-made buffalo-skin lodges. Each Apsáalooke could dress himself or herself in some of the finest examples of beaded buckskin leggings, shirts, dresses, and moccasins found among the peoples of the Great Plains. Apsáalooke horses remained a handsome prize through 1888, when the Blackfeet made the last attempt by Indians to capture them.

Acquiring horses from an adversary became the impetus for a system of acquiring social and political prestige. Known as "counting coup," the system involved the successful public challenging of an enemy. Four types of coup were generally recognized: touching a live opponent, taking an enemy's weapon during face-to-face combat, securing a picketed horse from an opponent's camp, and leading a horse raid against an adversary's camp.

Although taking an enemy's scalp lock was certainly proof of successfully challenging him, it was not accorded special honor. As Lowie recorded from one of his informants, "You will never hear a Crow boast of his scalps when he recites his deeds" (1983:218).

Furthermore, it was not the accumulation of booty that distinguished a warrior. It is true that the most prized of a warrior's possessions might be a bow or a horse taken from a Blackfeet, but property acquired from an enemy was often given to others, perhaps older than oneself, who were to be respected. The value of the coup lay primarily in the tremendous skill and daring needed to acquire it, as well as in the liberal disposition of the enemy's possessions among one's kinsmen and in the display of the acquired badges of merit. Ermine skins worn on a shirt and wolf tails attached to mocassin heels were among the badges worn with pride. At any public gathering, such as a feast or a dance, the moment of greatest excitement came when the warriors recited their coups, recounting their exploits and their skills. Coups afforded the opportunity for greater generosity, not for accumulation of goods.

While a man might be acknowledged for his hunting, curing, or storytelling abilities, only in counting coup could he be recognized as a "good man." Not to have gained even a single coup made a man a nobody. To have gained a single coup made him an honored person, and to have gained all four types of coup made him a chief. A chief was looked upon as a leader who ruled by example, not command, coordinating the camp's movement, mediating disputes between rival clans, and setting an example of generosity, honesty, skill, and bravery.

If Apsáalooke men characterized the volatile and dynamic elements in buffalo-day society, women represented the structural stability. While the men were out hunting buffalo and counting coup on the Cheyenne, attempting to enhance their social and political status, the women were maintaining the camp, nurturing the children, and caring for the sick and the aged. Women, however, joined in celebrating the battle achievements of their brothers and husbands. They also counted coup in their own way. Immediately following a buffalo hunt, with sticks in hand, women would rush to see who could be first to strike the fallen beasts.

Women were the owners of the family lodge. They tanned and sewed together the buffalo hides to make the tipi cover, repaired it when necessary, and took down the lodge and reerected it when the camp was moved. In matters affecting the operation of the family lodge, women were

## CHIEF LONG HAIR

One of the great chiefs is Long Hair. He's always successful against his enemies, leading numerous raids against the Blackfeet and Lakota and bringing back many horses and captive children. Even when Apsáalooke horses are captured by the Blackfeet or Lakota, with Long Hair around you know they're going to get 'em back. Whenever he goes out on a horse raid, he paints his face yellow with a red circle around it. It's his medicine, the Morning Star. Under his leadership the Apsáalooke prosper. But with the coming of the non-Indian and even though he signs a treaty in 1825 pledging mutual friendship with them, Long Hair foresees a day when these new people will so overwhelm the country that the Apsáalooke will greatly suffer.

He's called Long Hair because his hair grows so long, ninety-eight hands long. When he rides he never braids it. It's quite a sight to see. At night he sits in the middle of his lodge and his daughters comb out his hair in all directions. They then cut it so it wouldn't be any longer than ninety-eight hands. It must grow pretty fast. If his hair gets any longer, he'll die.

Long Hair lives to a good age. When he decides it's time, he tells his daughters not to cut his hair anymore. When it reaches a hundred hands long, Chief Long Hair passes on. This must be around 1840.

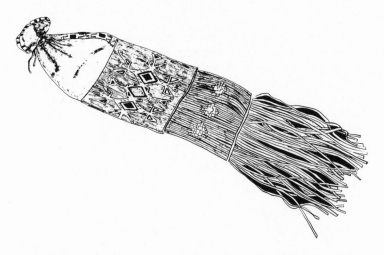

A beaded and quilled pipe bag within which the pipe and kinnikinnick are kept.

the decision makers. A woman's husband may or may not
have been successful in the hunt, but her contribution of
wild turnips, chokecherries, dried meat, and pemmican
prepared weeks in advance could always be counted on. In
the matrilineal clan system, kinship affiliation was traced
through the woman. She was also an artist, tailoring not
only all the buckskin clothing but embroidering the moccasins, leggings, shirts, and dresses with brightly colored
patterns of porcupine quills and, after trade with non-
Indians, beads. On rawhide parfleches she would paint col-
orful geometric designs. Women also were teachers, instructing children in their adult responsibilities and singing
them to sleep with stories of heroes, hunts, and the buffalo
days. When a son or daughter was troubled, he or she
would likely first seek out his or her mother or grandmother for advice. Women were the caretakers of the most
cherished and protective family possession, the medicine
bundle. They also sought visions in the mountains and ap-

plied spiritual gifts in doctoring the sick. They regularly took sweat baths and performed critical roles in the Sun Dance, the Tobacco Society, and other Apsáalooke religious expressions.

Despite the male-female role distinctions, an egalitarianism pervaded Apsáalooke world view. Men and women were equally eligible for social recognition and spiritual attainment. As in other Plains Indian societies, while the relationships and activities associated with medicine and family had strictly defined roles for both sexes, both men and women participated in and were affected by them. This equality has continued into the present. Both men and women receive the prayers of their clan uncles and aunts, both rely upon and use medicine, and, since the 1950s, both dance in the Sun Dance.

This egalitarianism is, in fact, embedded in the Apsáalooke language. In the construction of a sentence containing third-person pronouns, ("he," "she," or "it"), Apsáalooke does not distinguish the sex of the subject. The statement *baachichíilik* can be translated as "'he' [or 'she' or 'it'] is looking for something." Because of this lack of distinction, it is not uncommon for an Apsáalooke speaking in English inadvertently to use the wrong pronoun in referring to the subject—"Linda is such a great dancer that *he* always wins at powwow contests."

One aspect of Apsáalooke society, the clan system, resisted the changes brought on by the horse and has continued to resist change. It is the structure upon which the *áassahke* (clan uncle and aunt) relationship, discussed in chapter 3, necessarily depends. The Apsáalooke clan system has always been an anomaly for anthropologists. While still sedentary and horticulturally focused, peoples such as the Arapaho, the Cheyenne, and the Lakota had clan structures not unlike that of the Apsáalooke. Leadership roles, both political and religious, and property and land inheritance were clearly and rigidly designated through clan descent. With the arrival of the horse and the movement onto the northern plains, however, the clan structure proved too inflexible to accommodate the buffalo-hunting ecology.[6] Because the buffalo dispersed during the winter and gathered during the late-summer mating season, flexibility was needed in the social organization of the peoples who moved with the herds. Such tribes were usually made up of bands of individuals linked by voluntary association rather than by consanguinity, because the size of the bands could readily be adjusted to meet the changing circumstances brought about by the buffalo herds. Although they were as integrated with, and dependent on, the buffalo as any other nomadic plains people, the Apsáalooke alone retained their clan system.

This is not to suggest that the Apsáalooke clan system did not undergo changes. Whereas descent lines formerly had delineated political and religious offices, the system of ascribed status shifted to an emphasis on achieved rank. While clan affiliation and membership remained based primarily on consanguinial ties, additional flexibility became possible. The Apsáalooke institutionalized the practice of adoption. An individual born into a given clan could, at his or her discretion, change affiliation and be adopted by a different family and clan.

Fred Eggan, in his superb analysis and classification of Plains Indian social organizations, maintained that the Apsáalooke kinship and clan structures were a transitional system "in the process of changing from a pure Crow type, such as their close relatives the Hidatsa possess, to a 'Generational' type, such as the Cheyenne and Arapaho have developed" (1955:94). The question, however, of why the Apsáalooke clan system is so resilient remains to be answered. After all, the Apsáalooke preceded the Arapaho, Cheyenne, and Lakota onto the plains by several generations. Yet even the length of their involvement with the buffalo-hunting ecology was not enough to cause replacement of the clan structure.

[6] See Oliver (1962) for a discussion of the societal changes resulting from the movement of peoples into the plains ecology.

The resilience of the clan structure during the buffalo days may be related to its continuity today. Specifically, the need for interdependence and cooperation among members of a clan overshadowed the need for flexibility. While Apsáalooke society may have been pressed by the ecology of the buffalo, the presence of numerous adversaries, which continues today, provided a more immediate and dire concern. Furthermore, to the extent that the clan structure is a pivotal metaphor in the way the Apsáalooke see themselves, to relinquish the clan system would be to remove a critical and concrete image that is vital for Apsáalooke self-identity.

## The Yellow Eyes and the Reservation Days

The Apsáalooke encountered non-Indians for the first time in 1743, when they met two French explorers, probably in present-day northeastern Wyoming. These explorers, the La Vérendrye brothers, called the Apsáalooke *beaux hommes* (handsome men). This description was reiterated in 1832 by George Catlin, who considered the Apsáalooke

a handsome and well-formed set of men as can be seen in any part of the world. There is a sort of ease and grace added to their dignity of manners, which gives them the air of gentlemen at once. I observed the other day, that most of them were over six feet high, and very many of these have cultivated their natural hair to such an almost incredible length, that it sweeps the ground as they walk, . . . giving exceeding grace and beauty to their movements. [1973:49]

During this initial period of contact the term "Crow" was erroneously applied to the Apsáalooke. The misnomer may have resulted from a casual translation of the term Apsáalooke (although it means "large-beaked bird," the term does not refer specifically to a crow), or it may have resulted from observation of the hand gesture used in Indian sign language to refer to the Apsáalooke, which mimics the movement of a bird's wings. The name "Crow" has continued to be used, though not by the Apsáalooke when they

speak in their native language. The Apsáalooke term for
white person is *baashchíile*, literally meaning "person with
yellow eyes."

The Apsáalooke and the non-Indians characterized their
early relations with each other as "friendly." Under the
leadership of Chief Long Hair, the Apsáalooke signed their
first treaty, the Treaty of Friendship, with the U.S. government in 1825. In this treaty the government was acknowledged "supreme" relative to other foreign governments
and given the right to regulate trade and other contacts
between the Apsáalooke and non-Indians; for its part, the
government agreed to protect the tribe from unauthorized
intrusions into tribal country by non-Indians. In 1851 the
so-called Fort Laramie Treaty established the first boundaries of the Apsáalooke territory, an area in southern Montana and northern Wyoming, in the region of the Yellowstone River, totaling 38,531,147 acres (see map).

The territory was abundant in beaver and buffalo, and
beginning in the 1820s the Apsáalooke became important
links in a rapidly growing and prosperous fur trade. While
not active as trappers, the Apsáalooke did take part in the
exchange of finely tanned furs for European and American
manufactured goods such as guns, knives, kettles, dyed
cloth, and beads. Among all the furs shipped to eastern mar-
kets, Apsáalooke buffalo robes were particularly prized,
bringing a high price and, as a consequence, having a critical position in the Yellowstone fur trade (Heidenreich 1985:
10). The fur trade enhanced the Apsáalooke material culture and broadened the horizons of their world as they interacted with the non-Indian traders and trappers and the
other Indian groups who gathered at the annual rendez-
vous and at the fur companies' trading posts.

The fur trade, however, was short-lived. By the 1840s
the beaver population had been depleted, and within several generations the buffalo experienced a similar fate. But
the land of the Apsáalooke was still rich in natural resources, and other people would arrive to replace the traders and the trappers.

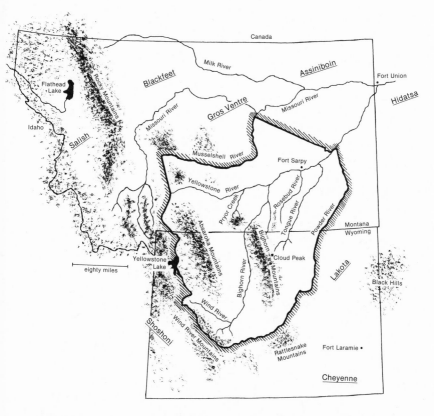

Apsáalooke Country, as established by the Fort Laramie Treaty, 1851 (state boundaries have been added for perspective).

The apparent calm of Apsáalooke life turned turbulent. The Yellowstone River valley was flooded with new groups of non-Indian immigrants, first by gold seekers in the 1860s, then by cattle ranchers, and, in the 1890s, by homesteaders searching for a new life. The Apsáalooke had been successful against the Blackfeet, the Cheyenne, and the Lakota, but they were less able to challenge the full and "friendly" onslaught of the *baashchíile*.

As a result of treaties, acts of Congress, and other land cessions to the government, the Apsáalooke witnessed the size of their once immense homeland diminish.[7] Another Fort Laramie Treaty was convened in 1868, and with Chief Blackfoot representing the Apsáalooke, the Crow Reservation was reduced to some 8 million acres. Soon after the treaty was signed, the first Crow Agency was established, near Livingston, Montana. The Apsáalooke had ceded the vast tracts of land in exchange for promised indemnities associated with their health, education, and welfare. For instance, the 1882 Act of Congress provided, in exchange for land, that the government would build housing and acquire livestock for the Apsáalooke. By 1905 the reservation boundaries had been reduced to approximately 2,282,000 acres. The land base has remained roughly the same since then. The present reservation is in south-central Montana, southeast of Billings (see map).

Contact with non-Indians also brought diseases against which the Apsáalooke had little natural resistance; along with the loss of land came a loss of population. In the early 1800s a series of smallpox epidemics reduced the Apsáalooke population from nearly sixteen thousand to approximately four thousand. Having regained some of their former population by the mid-1800s, the Apsáalooke were again struck by a series of smallpox epidemics, which reduced their number from nearly eight thousand to less than two thousand by 1870. Only since the 1950s has the population regained something near its previous size; in 1985 the number of individuals enrolled as members of the Crow Tribe was 7,340, approximately 4,500 of whom resided on the reservation.

During the 1880s the Northern Pacific Railroad finished laying rail along the northern tier of the reservation. The Apsáalooke and what they had to offer thus became more accessible to the rest of the United States. The railroad brought with it an eastern market for buffalo hides. In fact,

[7] See Smith (1986) for an overview of Apsáalooke land cessions.

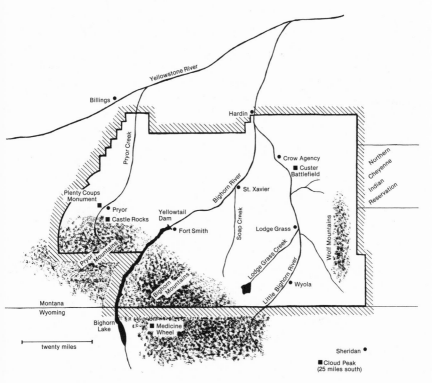

Crow Indian Reservation, 1987.

the Northern Pacific encouraged the slaughter of the vast herds. The more hides shipped, the greater the shipping revenues. Not long into the 1880s, however, the great herds of buffalo had vanished. And with the coming of the railroad, another flood of non-Indians swept Apsáalooke country. More homesteaders, missionaries, government agents—and liquor—found their way among the Apsáalooke.

The Allotment Act of 1887 had been intended to make farmers of the American Indians. Implicit in the act was the view that becoming an individual landowner was the first step toward becoming a farmer. Under increased pressure from non-Indian ranchers and farmers desiring additional lands, the government implemented the act on the Crow Reservation in 1905. Land not assigned to the Apsáalooke was opened up for non-Indian ownership. Vast tracts of land consequently passed from Apsáalooke control.

Government and Catholic boarding schools were soon established on the reservation. Students were forced to attend these schools, which offered a non-Indian curriculum taught only in English. In the Catholic schools, children caught speaking Apsáalooke were punished. In 1883 the Crow Boarding School opened near Crow Agency, followed in 1886 by the Saint Xavier Mission. The Carlisle Industrial School, of Pennsylvania, also began receiving Apsáalooke students in 1883. Additional Catholic schools were established near Pryor and on Lodge Grass Creek in the early 1890s.[8] Physically separated from family and culture, Apsáalooke children were taught an assemblage of values and skills not only alien but often contradictory to those held by their parents.

The Bureau of Indian Affairs (BIA), with the authority to fine, imprison, and withhold beef rations (there no longer were any buffalo to hunt), readily imposed its policies on the Apsáalooke. After all, only the Indians' "uncivilized" ways prevented them from becoming as successful as white farmers, or so the agents held. Attempting to eliminate all "barbarous acts," the 1884 Rules and Regulations of the Indian Office (BIA) "outlawed" and made it an "Indian offense" to hold a giveaway, a feast, a Sun Dance, or almost any other form of dance; to have more than one wife; to be a "medicine man"; to leave the reservation without permission; to consume alcohol; or to sell a horse to another Indian. The number of Apsáalooke horses had grown from fifteen thousand in 1880 to an estimated thirty to forty thousand by 1914, but by 1921 the number had been re-

---

[8] See Bradley (1982) and Watembach (1983) for histories of Catholic education on the reservation.

The building housing the Bureau of Indian Affairs at Crow Agency.

duced to less than one thousand. This reduction was partly the result of a series of severe droughts and theft by non-Indians, but more significantly, it was the result of a government policy of exchanging horses for cattle, sheep, pigs, and poultry. The rules also authorized the establishment of an "Indian Police Force," under the BIA's control, to enforce the provisions of the rules.

With off-reservation movement curtailed and a military force present to enforce the policy, intertribal warfare soon ceased. The last Apsáalooke horse raid took place in 1886. No longer could social and political status be acquired through counting coup. The system that had generated chiefs and male prestige no longer existed. With the passage of time positions of tribal leadership became confused, and an entire population of men found their traditional identity in question. With the end of intertribal warfare in the 1870s, the overt reason for holding the Sun Dance was also eliminated, and for several decades the "outlawed" ceremony was not held. The last buffalo-day Sun Dance took place in 1875.

Plenty Coups, Pretty Eagle, Medicine Crow, and a few others who had acquired the position of chief while it was still possible to do so, continued throughout the early part of the twentieth century to provide much-needed leadership. Their raids continued, no longer against the Blackfeet or the Lakota, but on Washington, D.C. Numerous Apsáalooke delegations met with government officials, attempting to secure concessions beneficial to the Apsáalooke. But with the passing of this generation of chiefs, the Apsáalooke found themselves in search of new sources of leadership.

One "raid" against the *baashchíile* was indeed a raid. In 1887, inspired by a vision received while participating in the Cheyenne Sun Dance, Wraps His Tail led an "outbreak" against the U.S. government. Claiming invulnerability from enemy bullets and promising a return to prosperity, Wraps His Tail and about sixty warriors "shot up" several buildings at Crow Agency and successfully eluded capture throughout the fall of 1887. In the confrontations that followed, several Apsáalooke and one government soldier were killed. But the raids and the claims of Wraps His Tail proved short-lived. While drinking from a river, Wraps His Tail was shot and killed by a Crow Indian policeman. His followers soon disbanded, and the "Crow outbreak" came to an end.[9]

Despite the imposition of government regulations, the Apsáalooke did not become "successful" farmers, nor did they stop consuming liquor. Neither, however, did they stop dancing. A spirit of defiance remained. The 1880s signaled the end of the buffalo days, as well as the freedom they entailed, and the beginning of an era of holding tight to what remained of the Apsáalooke dream.

[9]The account of Wraps His Tail, also known as Sword Bearer (a medicine saber was bestowed on Wraps His Tail during the Cheyenne Sun Dance), is elaborated in Calloway (1986).

In 1933, John Collier became commissioner of Indian affairs, and the policies of the BIA were set in a new direction. Under Collier's guidance the forced-assimilation policies of the previous century were largely reversed. The Indian Reorganization Act of 1934 repealed the Allotment Act and provided for the organization of Indian self-government and cultural revival. While electing not to adopt many of the specific provisions of the Indian Reorganization Act, the Apsáalooke did realize greater cultural, economic, and political sovereignty under the Collier initiatives. A constitution based on government by a general council was adopted in 1948. Every adult member of the tribe was given a vote in the council. A tribal constitution, court, and council of elected officers now governs many of the internal operations of the reservation. The regulations concerning "Indian offenses" were also abolished.

The Apsáalooke could once again publicly express their spirituality. In 1941, William Big Day sponsored the first Sun Dance held on the reservation in over sixty years. But the ceremony was not a resurrection of the buffalo-day Sun Dance. Big Day had gone to Fort Washakie, Wyoming, in 1938 and again the following year, participating on the second trip in the Shoshoni Sun Dance.[10] This was a significant undertaking and a turning point for Big Day. He received several visions, including one in which he saw a Shoshoni and an Apsáalooke greeting each other, right arms extended in friendship. In another vision, Eagle feathers used by John Trehero, the Shoshoni medicine man who "ran" the Sun Dance, were ceremoniously presented to Big Day (Voget 1984:133). Trehero had always had a close association with the Apsáalooke. He spoke their language, had an Apsáalooke half brother, and had visited the reservation several times, including trips made to doctor patients.

Under Trehero's tutelage, and with the strong support of Robert Yellowtail, the Crow Reservation superintendent

[10] See Voget (1984) for a complete and insightful discussion of the diffusion of the Shoshoni Sun Dance to the Apsáalooke.

and older brother of Tom Yellowtail, Big Day held a very well attended and successful Sun Dance near his home in Pryor in June, 1941. During the ceremony Trehero presented Big Day with the feathers of his vision and doctored people at the center pole, demonstrating the power of the Sun Dance. Once again the Apsáalooke had a meaningful way to offer prayers and gain access to spiritual power for guidance and health. Trehero remained active in both the Shoshoni and the Apsáalooke Sun Dances throughout the years that followed. In January, 1985, at over one hundred years of age, John Trehero passed on. Men such as Barney Old Coyote, Old Coyote's son Henry, Joe Hill, Tom Yellowtail, and, most recently, Larson Medicine Horse, Dan Old Elk, and John Pretty On Top have continued to guide the Apsáalooke through the Sun Dance.

Procedural differences exist between the buffalo-day and the contemporary forms of the Sun Dance, most notably in the motivation for sponsoring the dance and in the structure of the ceremonial lodge, but many Apsáalooke consider the contemporary form to be the same order of religious expression as its predecessor. That the name for the dance, *Ashkísshe*, literally meaning "imitation lodge," has remained the same is indicative of this similarity. Some have even maintained that both forms of the Sun Dance originated with Old Man Coyote.

Life is still turbulent for the Apsáalooke, however. Subtle and pervasive adversaries continue to confront them. The Apsáalooke must face high unemployment, widespread poverty, alcoholism, poor health, Christian Fundamentalist missionaries, and deep-seated prejudice. In the 1950s, under the threat of a government condemnation suit, the Apsáalooke were coerced to sell rights to much of the Bighorn Canyon so that a multipurpose dam could be built (Brooke 1981). The negotiations associated with what became known as the Yellowtail Dam project are a clear reminder of who retains ultimate sovereignty over the lives of the Apsáalooke.

In their dealings with Euro-Americans the Apsáalooke

## THE FIRST SUN DANCE

It's Old Man Coyote. He's traveling along one day when he begins to hear singing and whistling that's unfamiliar to him. He becomes curious about the sounds and looks around for their source. After a little while Old Man Coyote comes across an old buffalo skull and there underneath it are mice; they're singing and dancing and blowing little whistles. They're having a Sun Dance, just like what you'd see today. This is how Old Man Coyote learned of the Ceremony. He then gave the Sun Dance to the people.*

*This account of the Sun Dance origin was offered by an elder who had been associated with the Sun Dance for over forty years.

have always been rather pragmatic, guided in part by the visions of their great chiefs. Although the tribe's early contact with non-Indians was limited to traders, trappers, and a few government representatives, as early as the 1850s, Apsáalooke prophetic dreams foretold the coming of steamboats, railroads, airplanes, many-storied buildings, and countless numbers of non-Indians. In 1857, at the age of nine, the great chief Plenty Coups had a vision that revealed that the buffalo would disappear and be replaced by "spotted buffalo" (non-Indian cattle), an event that could not have been anticipated by either Indian or non-Indian at the time. Besides foretelling drastic changes, visions offered advice in dealing with the *baashchíile:* use your mind; those who have fought them have been beaten; learn from the small Chickadee, who is wise and listens to the mistakes of others, that you should establish peaceful relations with the non-Indian, for in the great forest of Indian peoples only the tall tree housing the Chickadee shall withstand the Four Winds, the rush of the non-Indian (Linderman 1962:73–74).

Lessons learned from the song of the Chickadee have contributed to the continued vitality of the Apsáalooke, as has their view of themselves and of their world. The Apsáalooke world view is predicated on the presence of turbulent waters. As the waters threaten, the driftwood lodges. The history of the Apsáalooke waters abounds with boulders, eddies, and fast currents; with the Blackfeet, the Lakota, and the *baashchíile;* and with poverty and prejudice. To whatever extent the Apsáalooke perceived turbulence in their waters, they will strive to lodge together, keeping their institutions tightly bound.

But the lodging of the driftwood is not inflexible. As the water's depth, speed, and course change, so too must the driftwood, if it is to remain lodged. Inherent in the world view and associated institutions of the Apsáalooke is a recognition of and accommodation to individual interpretation and expression. A consensus of view is seldom found in either the community or the individual (this accommodation to diversity is elaborated in chapter 8, "The Wagon Wheel"). The consequence of this flexibility is readily apparent in the changes the Apsáalooke have encountered and to which they have adapted. The resilience of the Apsáalooke and of such institutions as *áassahke* and *xapáaliia* can be credited in part to their unique vision of themselves and to their heeding the song of the Chickadee.

# CHAPTER 3

# Clan Uncle and Aunt (*Áassahke*)

TO BE ACKNOWLEDGED by others of the tribe as a participant in the world of the Apsáalooke, a person must "feast" his or her clan uncles and aunts (*áassahke*). Even if a person does not participate in traditional religion (Native American Church or Sun Dance), speak fluent Apsáalooke, or take part in powwows or even Crow Fair (an annual powwow, rodeo, and fair held on the reservation during the third weekend in August), the *áassahke* should be honored.

## The Clans

Apsáalooke society is divided into eight matrilineal clans (*ashammaléaxia*). This number is a reduction from the thirteen clans that existed during the buffalo days (Lowie 1983:9). As membership in a particular clan dwindled, its members merged with another clan, assuming that clan's name and depending on its support. The Ties-in-a-Bundle clan is the result of such a merger. The eight clans that have continued into the present are:

| | |
|---|---|
| Ashhilaalíoo | Newly Made Lodge |
| Ashshitchíte | Big Lodge |
| Úuwuutasshe | Greasy Mouth |
| Ashíiooshe | Sore Lip |
| Ashképkawiia | Bad War Deeds |
| Bilikóoshe | Whistling Water |
| Xúhkaalaxche | Ties-in-a-Bundle |
| Ashkáamne | Piegan |

Each clan's name is indicative of an event or a characteristic associated with its members, often having been assigned

## THE FOUR BROTHERS

Four brothers decide to worship in four different ways to see who will be the most successful and live the longest. One brother prays to the Sun. Every morning at sunrise, he's up and makes an offering to the Sun. The second man goes out to fast and thirst. He stays out sacrificing from one to four days at a time, returns to camp for a few days, and then fasts again. The third brother builds sweat lodges and calls men of importance to come in and sweat with him. The fourth man feasts and gives gifts to his clan uncles and aunts, men and women of his father's clan. Whenever a deer or buffalo is killed he feeds these people.

The faster becomes a prominent man, but is soon killed. The Sun worshiper becomes famous as well, but like his fasting brother, is killed. The sweat lodge owner lives to a good age, becomes a chief, and then dies. But the fourth brother, the one who feasts and gives gifts to his clan uncles and aunts, becomes a *great* chief and lives to such an age that "when he moves his skin tears." His deeds are the greatest. Since then, this practice of honoring our clan uncles and aunts has continued.*

* While the story of the four brothers is still told today, this informant's version is not nearly as embellished as that recorded by Lowie (1918:244–54).

Housing at Crow Fair.

by Old Man Coyote. For instance, one group of Apsáalooke persistently ate the fatty portions of their meat, rendering their mouths rather greasy. Old Man Coyote thus called them Úuwuutasshe (Greasy Mouth). In another example, a group of aspiring young men, upon returning from a horse raid, claimed great achievements and coups counted on the enemy. But the claims proved to be false, and the men were named Ashképkawiia, Bad War Deeds. Not only false boasts but also foolish actions continue to characterize the members of this clan. In one well-known story, also re- corded by Lowie (1983:16–17), the Apsáalooke fled camp at the onslaught of a Blackfeet raid, that is, all fled but one Ashképkawiia member, who chose to remain behind. As an enemy warrior began looking over some of the Ashképka- wiia's belongings, from his hiding place high in a tree the

Ashképkawiia yelled, "Stop that! Don't take those things!" He was, of course, immediately discovered and shot down, losing more than just his belongings. So it is with members of the Bad War Deeds clan.

Six of the clans are paired into three kindred groups. The members of each of these pairs of clans consider themselves related, as though they had been "raised in the same family." In the Pryor region, for instance, the members of the Ashhilaalíoo and Ashshitchíte clans are so closely allied that individuals of either clan consider themselves members of the other. While not as closely joined, the other paired clans are the Úuwuutasshe and Ashíiooshe and the Ashképkawiia and Bilikóoshe. Besides the brothers and sisters of one's own clan, those of one's allied clan can also be counted on to help keep the driftwood tightly lodged.

Keeping the driftwood lodged is precisely the goal toward which the clans strive. Although many functions formerly associated with the clans, such as clan exogamy and residential proximity, have diminished in importance, the cooperative character of the clan and its members has not. When an aspirant to a tribal council office is seeking support, his clansmen can be counted on for the money needed for a feed and a political rally and for votes at the election. At college graduation or the time of induction into the Tobacco Society, an individual can look to his or her fellow clan members for the Pendleton blankets, the food, the horses, and the money that will be distributed abundantly at the giveaway that marks the occasion. After the alfalfa has been cut and bundled, among those stacking the bales will be groups of clan brothers. Several weeks later, the same groups may camp together in the Bighorn Mountains and hunt for elk to help feed their families. When a fight breaks out in a Hardin bar, clan brothers who had not necessarily been "partying" together before the fight will come to one another's aid. There is a tendency to look to, and depend on, the members of one's clan in matters that affect one's social and material well-being. What the clan is (the resources it can muster and the ingenuity and cooperation of

Housing at Crow Agency.

its members), determines to a significant extent what the
individual can become.

Clan membership is based on affiliation with the women's
descent line from mother to daughter. All male offspring of
a matrilineal line are thus members of the same clan and
are classified as "brothers," differentiated only by relative
age. A man's older brother is termed *biiké*, while a woman's
older brother is referred to as *bisaalé*. A younger brother is
termed *bachuuké* by both a man and a woman. One's father
does not share membership in his own offspring's clan but
rather is a member of his mother's clan, in which he is an
older or younger brother of its members.

Correspondingly, all male members of one's father's clan
(one's paternal grandmother's clan), are considered "fathers," regardless of their age. The term by which such
clan members are called, however, varies, depending on
the sex of the speaker and on whether the term is used to
address or to refer to a person. While speaking directly

with a male member of one's father's clan, a man addresses him as *axée*, and a woman addresses him as *basaakáa*. Both terms translate as "my father." When talking about a male member of one's father's clan, a man refers to him as *biilápxe*, while a woman refers to him as *basáake*, both terms also meaning "my father." The English expression "clan uncle" is also used by either sex to address and refer to men of one's father's clan. In addition, the general term *áassahke* is used in referring to one's "clan uncles and aunts," the men and women of one's father's clan.

The reciprocal term of *áassahke* is *baakáate*. While an individual would refer to his or her clan uncles and aunts as *áassahke*, they would refer to him or her as *baakáate*, meaning "my child." This is a general term, designating reference to both sexes. Interestingly, it is also the term used to refer to the offspring of an animal.

The focus of the following discussion is on clan uncles and only minimally considers clan aunts. *Áassahke* will be used in this text to include the various terms for "my father" as well as to refer to one's "clan uncles and aunts."

## The Áassahke

A potentially enormous number of individuals bear the *áassahke* relationship to any given person. Because the entire Apsáalooke society is divided into eight clans (not all the clans are of equal size), and because each individual is necessarily aligned with one of these clans, each Apsáalooke has a large number of clan uncles and aunts. In many situations an individual is aligned with two clans, each a kindred of the other. In these instances the number of *áassahke* is substantially increased.

In practice, however, the number of *áassahke* is considerably lower than the number of individuals who qualify for the relationship. Those individuals consciously recognized and sought out among all who are classed as *áassahke* are the men and women who can best perform the functions associated with the *áassahke* role. Only a few people act in the capacity of *áassahke* for any given individual.

The *áassahke* relationship is based on reciprocal exchange between a "son" or a "daughter" and the clan uncle or aunt. In exchange for gifts of respect, feasts, and presents, an *áassahke* provides praise, prayer, and protection. A specific *áassahke* will be sought out on the basis of his or her ability to successfully and continually offer these gifts. These gift exchanges help solidify the social and spiritual fibers of the Apsáalooke world and, most importantly, the individual's niche within it.

The description of the *áassahke* relationship offered here is virtually identical to that given by Lowie (1912:201–202, 1983:20–21). Both describe the same sorts of exchanges between the same categories of kin. This pivotal kinship institution, like many other dimensions of Apsáalooke society, has thus remained fundamentally intact since the buffalo days.

## Like Medicine

Respect is offered to one's *áassahke* in various forms. An individual may meet a clan uncle in passing at a grocery store or a social gathering and give him a dollar, saying "Get something good to eat or drink." It is improper to walk in front of one's *áassahke* while they are seated at a public gathering. When an individual receives an honor, such as being elected to tribal council office, dancing in a first powwow, graduating from high school, returning from military service unhurt, or winning an arrow-throw championship, the individual will hold a giveaway (*ammaakée*), in which he or she offers gifts to his or her various *áassahke*. *Ammaakée* are usually held at powwows, at feasts involving the extended family, and at dance parades (*ashhéeleetaawaalissuua*), which are ceremonial dances through the camp on the last day of Crow Fair. Gifts given during an *ammaakée* may include Pendleton blankets and shawls, less expensive quilts and blankets, five- and ten-dollar bills, and, occasionally, a horse or two, all gathered together and publicly distributed to one's *áassahke*. After a Sun Dance and during the Crow Fair Powwow, all one's clan uncles and aunts in attendance

## GIFT EXCHANGE

The father has phoned his son's clan uncle, inviting him to a sweat
and a meal. Upon arriving that afternoon, the *áassahke*, along
with several other men, most older than himself, and who have
just arrived themselves, go down the path to the creek. There
among the tall willows is the sweat lodge. The fire has been
"cooking" the rocks for over an hour and the sweat can now begin. After undressing and with "switches" of willows in hand, all
enter. The thick layers of canvas door come down and the rocks in
their pit glow with the heat "captured" in them. As the dippers
of water "dance" upon the rocks, the lodge fills with a dense,
penetrating steam. The "switches" stir the air and "beat" the sore
shoulders and backs of those within. One after another, each
gives prayer for the boy whose father is "putting on" this sweat
and whose birthday it is. The *áassahke* speaks of the boy's good
health and asks that it might continue for another year. He speaks
of the name he has given the boy but a few years before, and asks
that its power continue to help this boy become that which the
words of the name describe. He prays for strength and honesty,
and for sincerity to be with his "son" always. After a cooling dip in
the creek and dressing, a fine meal waits back at the house. The
boy sits beside his *áassahke* as he continues his prayer over the
meal. Again he asks that health and sincerity be with the child. It
is indeed a fine meal, "steak with all the trimmings," more than
enough for all. And all have brought a great appetite. Cake and
ice cream top it off. Pleasant and informal conversation follows,
as the boy rejoins his brothers in a game of chase. Upon depart-
ing that evening the clan uncle is given a western-style shirt, a
carton of cigarettes and a word of thanks, *ahóo*, for his prayers.

At a giveaway during Crow Fair an "announcer" calls for the *áas-sahke* to receive their blankets.

are given gifts. A Christmas giveaway in 1901 involved 500 horses, 23 buggies, 200 shawls, 600 blankets, 800 quilts, 50 tents, 2 stoves, 1000 elk teeth, and coffee, tea, sugar, overcoats, shirts, and clothing exchanged between the Pryor and Bighorn district Apsáalooke (Bradley 1970:52). Sweat baths accompanied by feasts are given throughout the year to specially selected *áassahke*. A lavish meal is furnished, including steak, liver with fried fat, fried beef stomach (a delicacy), potatoes and gravy, fry bread, berry pudding, fruit pie, cake, watermelon, and cantaloupe, all in generous quantities. No matter what the form, respect is offered. The *áassahke* are considered to be "like medicine." They are powerful and must be treated properly. One never jokes with an *áassahke*, but shows deference and respect.

## Praise Song

As one individual said, clan uncles are one's "public-relations men." They praise their *baakáate* publicly so that all will hear of their good deeds and grant them prestige. At an arrow-throw or hand-game tournament, a clan uncle will sing "praise songs" as he dances before all in attendance, recognizing his *baakáate* for a deed. At a giveaway, a clan uncle may publicly call out his thanks for the gifts he has received and commend his *baakáate* as an outstanding person. At the traditional parade held each morning during Crow Fair, among the hundreds of participants dressed in their finest beaded dresses and outfits will be several clan uncles singing "praise songs" as they ride their best horses behind the honored person.

In Apsáalooke culture, it is considered improper for a person to "speak out about" himself or herself, to boast about his or her achievements in the company of others. When one is to be publicly recognized, another must mediate for him or her. One of the most respected Apsáalooke elders, despite his many and varied accomplishments as a Sun Dance leader and *akbaalía* ("one who doctors"), never discusses his own achievements; he seldom talks about himself but lets his wife do so in the presence of others. There are several reasons for this practice.

A clan uncle, a person older and more experienced than oneself, is more practiced in using words properly, and can thus better prevent their desecration. As will be discussed more fully below, for the Apsáalooke words have great

A woman is praised by her clan uncle during a morning parade at Crow Fair.

power, and their incorrect use, especially in public, can cause misfortune. In his public use of words, a clan uncle is similar to an "announcer," one who "owns the right" to speak publicly and who has medicine pertaining to the proper use of words. At a giveaway an "announcer" proclaims why the gifts are being given and who is to receive them. At the raising of the center pole for the Sun Dance Lodge, men who have served their country in war and have returned "without a scratch" are asked to share their "good fortune" and to wish similar success on the upcoming ceremony. The veterans, however, do not publicly recite their own war deeds. They relate them first to "one with the right," and "the announcer," with exactness and a tremendous vigor, transmits the words of the "good fortunes" to those present. At the installation of a newly elected tribal chairman, an "announcer" mediates much of the ceremony. An "announcer" is like a clan uncle. Both have the knowledge of "good words" and know how to use them properly. An individual dares not try to speak out without such knowledge.

Besides possessing knowledge of the proper use of words, the clan uncle should have certain other qualities if he is to recount one's good deeds. Although Apsáalooke men are no longer able readily to demonstrate their abilities and acquire status through acts of counting coup, they still aspire to positions of honor, which are characterized by certain ideal qualities.[1] A clan uncle should exhibit these qualities. He should be recognized as an honest and sincere person, a person called *bachéem* ("a man") by others. He is a "family man" with a "good home," perhaps with several children, all of whom show respect toward others. In his dealings with family, friends, and even strangers, he is known as a "generous person." Upon arriving at his house, one is always offered a cup of hot coffee. He has a "well-used sweat" and regularly offers the prayer and the pleasure of the sweat-bath ritual to others. To be *bachéem* is to be "dependable" in one's obligations and in one's word. When the clan uncle is esteemed by others, his public announcements are given greater legitimacy. Among one's various clan uncles, a young unmarried man known for his drinking

---

[1] Though not formalized, as the system of counting coup was, the deeds accomplished by veterans of foreign wars (World War II, Korea, and Vietnam) and the veterans themselves are still acknowledged and held in honor by the Apsáalooke. On horseback and proudly carrying the American and the Crow tribal flags, two veterans lead the morning parade at Crow Fair. When the center pole of the Sun Dance Lodge is about to be raised, a veteran comes forward to "wish the good fortune" experienced in a distant war upon those participating in the ceremony.

and pursuit of women is not a good candidate to be asked to speak out for one.

Perhaps the underlying rationale for a clan uncle's singing of a praise song is that it is an act of public declaration, an acknowledgment that each individual is linked to others and can attain social distinction only through them. One achieves honors not through one's efforts alone but through the aid offered by others, such as a clan uncle. Public praise is as much an acknowledgment of the aid rendered by the *áassahke* as it is a recognition of an individual's achievements.

## Prayer

While the public proclamation of a deed can be thought of as social mediation, the *áassahke* is also responsible for spiritual mediation. Besides announcing a deed, clan uncles also request that a blessing be bestowed on an individual. This mediation is in the form of a prayer, usually directed to the Maker. Depending on his own religious affiliation, be it Baptist, Roman Catholic, Christian Fundamentalist, Native American Church, Sun Dance, or any combination thereof, the *áassahke* prays for the individual in his own manner. Although nearly all Christian Fundamentalists, such as the Pentecostals, reject as "devil-worship" most expressions of Indian culture, especially traditional religion, many nevertheless observe the *áassahke* system and offer prayer when asked to.

As with social mediation, the particular *áassahke* chosen to give a prayer is an individual especially attuned to and involved in religious life and recognized as such by others. Perhaps he has a powerful medicine bundle, serves on a Catholic parish council, or is a preacher in the Foursquare church. At any rate, a conscious selection is made concerning who will offer spiritual mediation for an individual.

An *áassahke* may offer a prayer for an individual in many situations. For example, a birthday celebration is given for a member of the family, and an *áassahke* is invited to cut the cake. As he does, he gives a prayer for the honored person. In other instances there may be a specific need, such

Besides cigarettes, the pipe and kinnikinnick are often used in prayer.

as recovery from an illness, safety while on a long trip, or guidance in making a decision, and an *áassahke* will be asked to come and give prayer in a sweat. If a mother has a dream in which her child suffers misfortune, such as a car accident, a fight, or an illness, she may invite an *áassahke* of the child to the home, give him a feast, a pack of cigarettes, a blanket, possibly some money, and a sweat. In turn, the *áassahke* prays for the child. He may even recall a good dream of his own. After relating the benefits expressed in the good dream, the *áassahke* wishes for similar good fortune for the child. In another instance, a man who has had a "close call" in an automobile accident, escaping with only a minor injury, asks his clan uncles to his home for a feast and to receive gifts. The *áassahke* pray that no further injury results from the accident. As a Sun Dance draws to a close, clan uncles can be seen giving prayer for those who have "blown the whistles" and danced in the three-day ceremony.

On all future occasions of prayer—in a sweat, at a feast, before a meal, at the close of a day—the *áassahke* will acknowledge the gifts and ask that "good things" be bestowed on the giver.

### Protection

In addition to rendering social and spiritual mediation, the *áassahke* can offer direct gifts in exchange for those given to him: he can offer various forms of protection.

## THE ÁASSAHKE'S PRAYER

The water, still cool from a nearby spring and blessed at the center pole, has just been drunk. The Sun Dance fast is over. Not far from where the prayer for the water has been given, another prayer is about to be said. Facing east, a young man, one who has "blown the whistle" and "danced hard," is to receive words of prayer from his clan uncle. The old man, one who has also "danced hard," stands immediately behind his "son." With eyes closed and arms outstretched over the shoulders of the young man, the *áassahke* speaks of the sincerity just given and of the needs of one who's suffering. The prayer is given to Akbaatatdía, the One Who Has Made Everything, and to the particular Iilápxe, spirit Fathers, of the *áassahke*. All those who danced are also receiving similar prayers and blessings from their clan uncles and aunts. The young man's grandmother has brought him a blanket a short time before, and now at the close of the prayer it's given along with *ahóo* to his *áassahke*.

For the Apsáalooke, all words possess power, and an Indian name is particularly so endowed. An Indian name may be bestowed as an indication of the kind of life or a particular ability desired for a child. A name may reflect the good deeds of another or a particular experience that was beneficial and the desire that that experience or ability be with the child. Some children have been named for an outstanding person with the wish that the child will also receive the good fortune associated with the name. In an evening ceremony involving an opened medicine bundle, the incense of sweet cedar, blessed water, Eagle feathers, and gift exchange, an infant may be given a name such as Dwarf Woman. This name refers to the Little People, who inhabit various mountainous areas throughout Wyoming and Montana, and expresses the desire that the young girl will be as "strong as a Dwarf."

Because a name has spiritual power (*baaxpée*), if it is used properly and never taken in vain, it can help its recipient achieve a desired future. Following a naming ceremony, an *áassahke* might express the hope that the name will "agree with the child." If it does, the child will grow up strong and healthy. Should the name not agree with the child, the child may become sickly and needy. In such a case a new name would be asked for.

In addition to the respected elders and *akbaalía* (medicine men), the *áassahke* are frequently asked by a child's parents to name their child. After the naming ceremony, gifts are given for what has been bestowed.

Not only does a child depend on the *áassahke* for a name, but once it has been given, a child also depends on the name itself. Throughout his or her life a person may attribute his or her achievements, such as being elected to a tribal office, winning a powwow dance contest, or returning from Vietnam with honor, to the power of his or her Indian name. One often hears an Apsáalooke say, "I didn't do it on my own, but with the help of my name."

In the rather well known and humorous account of Joe Stinks, a rodeo bronc rider, the relationship of a person's

## JOE STINKS

Joe is a *bad* bronc rider. There's no two ways around it. The moment the chute opens he's on the ground. And then there's his name, Joe Stinks. What kinda name is that? His name is as bad as he is on horses.

Well, Crow Fair is comin' up and everyone will be there. It's our pride and joy. Folks will come from all over the country to see it. We want to show off our best. But then there's Joe!

So some of us get a few bucks together and give it to Joe and tell him to go down to the county courthouse and change his name. Maybe that'll help him. At least his name won't be so bad.

The big day is here. Hundreds of people are in the grandstands, many coming from as far away as Arizona and Alberta, Canada. "Out of chute number four, representing the great Crow Nation, . . ." and all his friends are anticipating the change in Joe, at least his name, "comes Joe . . . Stinks No More." But he hits the ground in record time anyway.

name to his or her ability is well illustrated. With a change
of name, a change in behavior is anticipated.

Besides naming a child, an *áassahke* can offer protection
through proper guidance. When a child is doing something
that may harm another in some way, an *áassahke* may give
advice, even though it is not necessarily sought by the
youth. Such guidance generally concerns the formation of
values and the ideal way a person is to conduct himself or
herself. The advice is seldom practical, such as advice on a
particular economic transaction.

The *áassahke* relationship generally does not involve
economic cooperation or monetary exchanges (other than
the giveaway gifts). Such transactions fall to fellow members of a clan and are a clan responsibility. As an *áassahke*
seeks to protect his "son" or "daughter," however, such
transactions may occur. One young man, troubled by dis-
satisfaction with his work and his relationships with women
and prone to drinking, was given fifty acres of good farm-
land and an offer of a house to help "settle him down." Such
help, while not the normal pattern, does occur.

### *Áassahke and World View*

The *áassahke* relationship encompasses and expresses the
"driftwood" world view. For the gifts of respect one offers—
the Pendletons, the meals, and the dollar bills—one's *áassahke* reciprocate with public praise, with prayers for health
or for assistance in an emergency, with the power of a name,
and with moral guidance. One's actions, and certainly one's
achievements, are significantly affected by the social and
spiritual mediation of one's *áassahke*. Through them a young
man or woman can be linked with that which is pervasive
and omnipotent, with the transcendent.

Traditional dancing at
Crow Fair Powwow.

# CHAPTER 4

# Medicine (*Xapáaliia*)

THE STORY OF "The Old Man's Medicine" exemplifies the Apsáalooke world view. The "old man's" identity and focus are not so much on himself as on that of which he is a part—his relationship with the Rattlesnake, one of his spiritual Fathers. The Rattlesnake is an ally, not an adversary. While engaged in dialogue with the Rattlesnake, the "old man" and it and the world are in balance as equal partners. The "old man's" sacrifices in previous Sun Dances and the respect he has shown the Rattlesnake throughout his life are reciprocated by a power to cure sickness. Because he is an *akbaalía* (one who doctors), the old man and others are transformed by the spiritual energy that transpires through the Rattlesnake, by what is often called "medicine" in English and referred to as *baaxpée* (spiritual power) and as *xapáaliia* (the tangible representation of *baaxpée*) by the Apsáalooke.

The character of medicine presented here is from the perspective of the Sun Dance (Ashkísshe) religion. Certainly, other perspectives exist among the Apsáalooke. Members of the Native American Church or adherents of Roman Catholicism, both dynamic and vital segments of Apsáalooke religious expression, may hold alternative views. Even within the Sun Dance religion, with its emphasis on the personal vision experience, there is no strict consensus. The ritual process of committing oneself to a private vow, then seeking, acquiring, and, finally, applying spiritual power and meaning, is the essence of the Apsáalooke Sun

## THE OLD MAN'S MEDICINE

The "old man" must have walked this path to his hay field a hundred times or more, yet each time he catches a glimpse of something new. The sights, sounds, and smells of spring are all about. The path takes the man across a dry creek bed, where an old companion waits, resting his body on a large rock, warmed by the afternoon sun. As the "old man" crosses, the sounds of a hiss and a rattle greet him, stopping him in his tracks. With a few kind words a conversation begins, and the rattling soon subsides. The man bends over and with great respect lifts the coiled body of the Rattlesnake. Holding him in his arms near his face, he continues the dialogue. As a man that could "run" a Sun Dance, as an *akbaalía*, he's often seen with his old friend curled around his arm as he "charges" the forked tree of the Big Lodge. The power and strength of the Snake are part of the "old man's" medicine; it's one of his Fathers.

Dance religion. Group philosophy and shared symbolism are subordinate to the individual's interpretation of, and relationship to, the transcendent and to the quality known as *baaxpée* and manifested as *xapáaliia*. The Sun Dance religion is concerned not so much with prescribing a conception of the spiritual as with offering a means to attain it. It is a facilitative, rather than a prescriptive, religion. There are, however, certain parameters within which the Sun Dance participant achieves his or her own vision of and realization within the spiritual. These parameters have shown significant resilience throughout time. With only a few exceptions, the means of acquiring, the ways of applying, and the fundamental character of *xapáaliia* have remained consistent with those expressed during the buffalo days and recorded by Lowie (1922c and 1983) and Wildschut (1975).

## Power (Baaxpée)

As Lowie observed, *baaxpée* "is primarily an expression of power transcending the ordinary" (1922c:317). This power certainly has a manifest dimension, which human beings can observe and experience. The noun *xapáaliia* refers to the tangible representation of *baaxpée*, as in the Eagle-feather fan, the Otter skin, and the Buffalo effigy assembled in a medicine bundle. Such objects, revealed as a bundle is opened, symbolize specific attributes of *baaxpée*. The *xapáaliia* is a channel through which the *baaxpée* flows. The *baaxpée*, in turn, flows from the transcendent. The essence and efficacy of medicine thus resides not in the manifest but in a power "transcending the ordinary."

Nevertheless, it is in the manifest, in the ability to transform objects and lives, that the power of medicine is affirmed. Medicine can effect a cure and preserve a life, or it can withhold life. Medicine influences people in their daily transactions and in moments of dire need. The term *baaxpée* has an additional connotation in that it can refer to an individual "on the right side," i.e., a member of the political faction currently controlling the tribal government and thus a recipient of "all the benefits." Such an individual

The Little Bighorn River, between Crow Agency and Lodge Grass, Montana.

might find himself or herself in line for a position as game warden or eligible for new housing. To have *baaxpée* is to have "good luck." *Baaxpée*, in all its meanings, implies linkage with a power that is greater than the mortal self, a power which can benefit the self and upon which the self depends.

But *baaxpée* is more than the power to alter a path, effect a cure, or obtain a job. It is also the power to know which path should be taken. A decision needs to be made, or maturity needs to be obtained. *Baaxpée*, expressed through a dream or a vision, can offer wisdom. The wisdom can resolve a temporary indecision, or it can bring forth an entire world view. For at least one *akbaalía*, whom I will discuss in chapter 8, *baaxpée* has defined a design for living and an understanding of the world.

*Baaxpée* is a link to the ultimate life-force, on which all phenomena depend, and to the perennial meaning in all phenomena. It is also the power that transforms objects and lives. It ushers life-force and meaning into the lives of the Apsáalooke. The transformation itself becomes an indication of the direction, meaning, and vitality of *baaxpée*. The term *xapáaliia* refers not only to the contents of a medicine bundle but also to the objects and lives that are touched by the contents and, thus, by *baaxpée*. That which is transformed becomes *xapáaliia*.

### The One Who Has Made Everything (Akbaatatdía)

According to many Apsáalooke, medicine is ultimately derived from and sanctioned by Akbaatatdía, the One Who Has Made Everything. Though called by a variety of names—the First Doer (Iichíkbaalee), the One Above (Báakukkule), Father (Axée), Old Man Coyote (Isáahkawuattee), or the Old Man (Isáahka)—the Maker is nevertheless conceptualized as distinct and omnipotent. One addresses the Maker in daily prayer and in the vow before a three-day fast. The Maker is the ultimate recipient of, and respondent to, all requests and pledges. If the gift of a vision is bestowed during a fast, it transpires from the Maker's will. Similarly, the power to doctor an afflicted person originates from the Maker. The power and wisdom of *baaxpée* emanate from the transcendent, from Akbaatatdía.

Unlike the Euro-American notion of a single, anthropomorphic deity, the Apsáalooke Maker is conceived of as more diffuse and less humanlike. Akbaatatdía is neither a loving nor a vengeful deity. Akbaatatdía does not project an established morality that all must obey; therefore, It does not hold supremacy over all human beings or exact retribution for mortal transgressions. Akbaatatdía is more appropriately conceived of as a pervasive agent, omnipotent over all natural forces, yet part of all natural forces, the ultimate life-force, and the perennial meaning in the cosmos. The

## XAPÁALIIA

Among those at the door of the Big Lodge is a non-Indian woman who begins very loudly to ridicule and taunt those within. Her actions upset many and distract most from their intent. And then it happens. One of the dancers "takes a hard fall," is given a vision. He lies there as if lifeless. This is too much for the woman; she really starts in now. "That man is dying. Call in a doctor. Stop this dance." Fearing that the woman may disrupt what the man is receiving, an *akbaalía* makes his way to the center pole. He prays with his Eagle feathers for power. Once the power is received, the feathers are pointed at the woman. She immediately collapses. It must be the heat, some think. She is taken to the shade of a nearby tree and attempts are made to revive her, all unsuccessfully. Finally the *akbaalía*, a man who can never use his gifts to permanently harm another, comes to her side. He "touches" her with the Eagle feathers. She immediately awakes and for the remainder of her stay at the Sun Dance, remains quiet, not doubting that sought by the dancers.

Lakota concept of Wakan-Tanka, the pervasive Great Mysterious, approximates the character of Akbaatatdía (Walker 1917 and Brown 1953).

### Father (*Iilápxe*)

Though Akbaatatdía is considered the ultimate source of *baaxpée*, medicine is always mediated through an Iilápxe, which literally means "his Father." In one sense, the Maker has never revealed Itself directly as a distinct entity to mortal human beings. When a faster receives a vision from Akbaatatdía, it is an Ililápxe, such as the Buffalo, the Eagle, the Otter, or the Sun, that serves as the instrument of mediation, the personal instructor, the guide. One who is praying often addresses both Akbaatatdía and the specific Iilápxe of his or her vision. An *akbaalía* usually prefaces a doctoring session with prayer to "his Fathers." *Baaxpée* is channeled from Akbaatatdía through the Iilápxe. The Iilápxe and the associated *xapáaliia* thus provide an opening to the spiritual.

The revealed character of a spiritual Father is considered part of the natural world. The Apsáalooke concept of Iilápxe thus has parallels to the Lakota concept of Akicita Makon, or "sacred messengers." Like their Apsáalooke counterparts, Akicita Makon comprise both animate and inanimate agents within nature (Walker 1917:79). The Buffalo and the Rock exemplify such agents. As a medicine bundle is opened, the objects revealed might include animal furs (elk, ermine, otter), rocks of various shapes and sizes, sweet grass, and feathers (eagle, flicker, hawk). The contents of a medicine bundle, the tangible images of *baaxpée* and the symbols of one's Iilápxe, are expressions of the natural world. Indeed, the overall character of the Iilápxe suggests that *baaxpée* has a permeating, diffuse quality not unlike that of Akbaatatdía. Any natural object can be an extension of Akbaatatdía: the Sun and Stars, the Birds and Animals, even the Earth and Rocks on which one walks. While Akbaatatdía may never reveal Itself directly, as distinct from Its creation, It does reveal Itself as part of Its creation, in

The Elk, Iichíilikaashe

the form of an Iilápxe. *Xapáaliia* and Iilápxe are both extensions of the same being, Akbaatatdía. The distinction
between Akbaatatdía and Iilápxe is fundamentally one of
degree; each has a different level of transcendence from the
material world. The Iilápxe are thus the immediate and
personalized mediators for the more pervasive and transcendent Akbaatatdía.

Because the Sun Dance religion recognizes, and even
encourages, individual interpretation and realization within

the spiritual, no dissonance generally arises when individuals hold contrasting understandings of the nature of the cosmos. The Apsáalooke may disagree among themselves on such issues, but the need for a consensus on cosmology is subordinate to the function of the religion as a means to the spiritual. Thus, as in the Apsáalooke conceptualization of the Maker, a diversity of views also exists on the specific character of the medicine mediators.

Some make a clear distinction between Akbaatatdía and Iilápxe, while others maintain that the Iilápxe are extensions of the Maker and not fundamentally distinct from It. The trickster-creator figure of Old Man Coyote is pivotal in some people's conception of the spiritual and its agents, while for others he is marginal, his adventures nothing more than humorous stories to be told during a sweat bath. Likewise, while many Apsáalooke refer to their medicine mediator as Iilápxe (one prominent *akbaalía* uses the English phrase "Medicine Father" to designate his), many others emphasize a less personal dimension, simply applying the term *xapáaliia* to this agent. The terms Iilápxe and "Father" are used interchangeably here to refer to medicine mediators.

The Apsáalooke tend to associate particular attributes of natural objects, such as great physical endurance or keen eyesight, with the character of the Iilápxe and, consequently, with the capabilities of the medicine itself. For instance, one individual possesses Squirrel medicine; the Squirrel is his Father. Because the squirrel has the foresight to store the nuts and berries needed by its family during the coming winter, Squirrel medicine assures one that food will be provided for one's family. Another person has acquired the power of the Mole or, specifically, of the dirt that the mole pushes as it tunnels its way into the earth. This dirt was once a barrier to free movements. By administering the "Mole's dirt," one with the power of the Mole curtails the flow of internal bleeding, nosebleeds, or hemorrhaging. The elk is one of the strongest, most admired animals; some suggest he is "king of all creatures." One who has Elk medicine can elicit the strength of the Elk. The quality that an object or animal manifests in the natural world parallels the power of the medicine represented by the Iilápxe.

One class of spirit helpers, which Euro-Americans generally do not recognize as part of the natural, or perhaps any other, world is the Awakkulé, or "Little People," who live in colonies in remote mountainous regions. One colony is said to live south of Pryor, near the Castle Rocks. During the buffalo days travelers made offerings, such as beads, to this particular group of Dwarfs so that they could anticipate a safe journey. When an expectant mother desired to know the gender of her child, she would leave two toys, one commonly associated with a boy and the other with a girl, at a particular site along Pryor Creek. Upon returning to the site the next day, she would find only one toy remaining. Whichever sex the toy was associated with would indicate the baby's sex.

Vividly remembered in the oral literature of the Apsáalooke, the Little People still make themselves known to humans.[1] While an Apsáalooke is in the Bighorn Mountains hunting deer, the Awakkulé may "pay a visit" by wandering into camp or confronting the hunter along the trail. The Little People may reveal a medicine to someone during a vision. The great chief Plenty Coups was adopted and aided by the Little People as well as by the Chickadee during one of his fasts. The actual "owner" of the Sun Dance Lodge is one of these Little People, known as the Little Old Man. He sits in the crotch of the forked center pole throughout the dance, watching and judging who among the fasters is sincere. The common expression "strong as a Dwarf" reflects the power that can be bestowed by Awakkulé on one who is judged worthy.

If the gift of medicine is to be used to aid human beings, it must be cared for and respected. During the initial vi-

---

[1] Lowie (1918) offers several accounts of the Dwarfs.

## THE LITTLE PEOPLE

A married couple in their mid-sixties decides to visit a close friend, an *akbaalía* known to have been adopted by the Little People. Because John doesn't have room to house his guests, after a good visit that evening the couple beds down in their truck camper for the night. The husband, being a rather conscientious man, puts the truck in gear, sets the emergency brake, and locks the cab doors. After a long day's journey the couple are ready for a good night's rest and fall fast asleep. But early in the morning hours, while it's still dark, their sleep is disturbed. The pickup is rocking back and forth. "Stop that, John, stop playing a trick on us. We want to sleep now." John is well known for his mischievous ways. But no voice from outside responds and the rocking soon subsides. When the couple awakes the next morning and step out of their camper, they find themselves in a field, several hundred feet from where they had parked the truck the evening before. The truck is turned in a direction opposite to what it had been, still in gear, brake set, and cab doors locked. John says, "It's the Little People; they've played a trick on you. They're the ones who picked you up and moved you." A colony of the Dwarfs live in the vicinity of John's house.

sion, or in subsequent ones, as the nature of the medicine is revealed to a faster, certain instructions and taboos may be communicated along with ways of honoring the medicine. A recipient of Elk medicine, for example, was instructed not to eat the heart of an elk. When that person uses the power of the Elk on another, as in doctoring, he insists that the afflicted one also not consume the elk's heart. A recipient of Buffalo medicine, for another example, was instructed that to eat any part of the buffalo would show disrespect for his Buffalo Iilápxe.

In addition to various dietary taboos, other restrictions are often imposed. One might offend one's Father by participating in hand games or other gambling events. Another might be prohibited from discussing the character of his or her medicine. A medicine object is always wrapped in a cloth or kept in some kind of pouch or container. It is never exposed to mundane or polluting influences. Under no circumstances is a medicine bundle opened in the presence of a menstruating woman. If such an accident occurs, the medicine must be reconsecrated in the incense of sweet cedar and prayed over by an *akbaalía*. Whenever a medicine is used, as in prayer or doctoring, it is first smudged with sweet grass or cedar. This incensing of the objects consecrates and "renews" them. Medicine demands the utmost respect.

Respect toward one's medicine necessitates its use only for "good purposes." Should its power be directed negatively toward others to cause sickness or deprivation, "bad medicine" is involved. The verb *áannutche* refers to the act of using "bad medicine." *Áannutche* literally means "to take the arm," as when one removes something that is vital to another. "To take the arm" is to cripple someone, making him or her susceptible to harm. The consequences of such an offense are often the withdrawal of the perpetrator's Iilápxe and the loss of spiritual power. Other equally serious losses can follow. For example, a close relative or a child may become "sickly." Some instances have been noted in which the user of bad medicine became ill and soon died.

The Wolf Mountains, east of Lodge Grass.

As one *akbaalía* mentioned, "Bad medicine always comes back to you. That's the pay you get for hurting people."

The foreknowledge that "bad medicine will come back to you" does not, however, hinder its use. Caution is often taken not to discard a broken fingernail or hair trimmings carelessly because another might acquire them and "make bad medicine." A fingernail, a spider, or a small stone can be "shot" by the power of the medicine and lodged in the back of one's neck, causing illness. These and other techniques of "bad medicine" are often blamed for a gradual decline in a person's health. The protection offered by a family's medicine bundle or, in severe cases, by an *akbaalía* is the sole means of counteracting "bad medicine" and restoring good health. "Bad medicine" is a very real threat to the safety of an individual.

The relationship between one's medicine mediator and oneself is that of a father to a child. Each instance of prayer reiterates this paternal linkage, because reference is often

## BAD MEDICINE

It's late evening of the last night of powwow dancing at Crow Fair. Only three fancy-dancers remain in the dance arena as several hundred look on. One will be judged the best, gaining social recognition and prestige, as well as five hundred dollars prize money. To the left of the dancers and around their drum, the singers begin. Each contestant dances with intensity and vigor, as bodies and feathers merge with the beat of the drum. At the height of the movement and song, one of the dancers "pulls up lame," his leg cramped beneath him. He limps to the benches and sits out the rest of the competition. He's been "shot" in the leg by one, perhaps jealous of his abilities, perhaps fearful of losing to him.

made to an Iilápxe, a Father. Whether human or spiritual, a father's role is to guide his child as well as to be an ally and a source of strength. The Iilápxe offer direction and aid and are always willing to listen to their "childrens'" needs and to stand by them. In fact, many Iilápxe stand within one as part of a newly extended existence; the Eagle may live in the chest of the *akbaalía.*

In this relationship the child never supplants the father. An adopted child is always dependent, because medicine "belongs" not to the mortal but to the spirit mediator. One has a "right" to spiritual power only for as long as the adoptive relationship exists, and then only through the mediation of the guardian Father. Medicine is simply "on loan."

## *Transcendence (Baaxpée)*

Medicine may be associated with physical properties, but it always transcends them. This notion is suggested by the term *baaxpée,* which means "power that transcends the ordinary." The terms *xapáaliia* and *baaxpée* are both based historically on the element *xapaa,* which no longer occurs in the language as a free form (Matthews 1977). Lowie suggests the same conceptual basis in both terms, evidenced by the element *xp* (1922:315–16). In any case, the *baaxpée* is conceived of as entailing spiritual properties.

The transcendent quality of medicine can be illustrated by a drink administered by one prominent *akbaalía.* The "brew," as it is called, is derived from a particular bush that grows on the slopes of a Wyoming mountain. It is prepared by boiling the plant in water. Those who seek the assistance of the *akbaalía* are often supplied with a jar of the bitter-tasting "brew" and instructed to drink a certain amount regularly to alleviate their affliction, whether it be the effects of a stroke, diabetes, or a cold. In the treatment of diabetes, the "brew" is particularly effective.

Because diabetes is widespread among the Apsáalooke, as it is among many other American Indian populations, a diabetic will often initially seek out the "cure" of the Indian Health Service (IHS) physician. A rigid diet, regular checkups, and, possibly, insulin injections are prescribed, all much to the despair of the patient. Dietary restrictions are understandably viewed with reluctance in a society in which meals and feasting are intricately woven into the social etiquette and play a critical role in the *áassahke* relationship. After a trial period, usually not longer than a few weeks, the non-Indian remedy may be "judged a failure" by the diabetic. He or she may then seek out the *akbaalía* known for his "brew." After offering prayer and doctoring the patient with his Eagle-feather fan, the *akbaalía* will give the patient the "brew."

In more than one instance, an IHS physician has continued regular testing of the patient's blood-sugar levels, knowing that the treatment has been abandoned. Much to the physician's amazement, the blood-sugar level has returned to normal. On one occasion an IHS physician knew that the activities of the *akbaalía* were involved. Curious and hoping to find a treatment that would be more acceptable to the Indian patients, the physician sought out the *akbaalía*.

When asked whether he would divulge the source of his treatment, the *akbaalía* responded with a polite but unequivocal no. In the first place, he explained, the "brew" was not his to give in such a manner, since it belonged not to him but to his Iilápxe. Only his Iilápxe could determine the manner in which the medicine should be applied. More important, for the medicine to be effective it could not be administered solely on a mundane basis. The plant used in the "brew" could, of course, be ascertained through persistence by the IHS physician, but the "brew's" effectiveness was not derived strictly from its chemical composition. Rather, the *baaxpée* within the drink had cured the diabetic. Needless to say, the spiritual quality of medicine is considered by the Apsáalooke to be unintelligible to the IHS physicians with their orthodox medical training.

Another context in which *baaxpée* is exhibited is in the "pulsating" of Eagle feathers. After a prayer during a prayer meeting or while standing in front of the center pole at a

An Eagle feather trimmed with ermine fur and horse hair.

Sun Dance, the *akbaalía* "touches up" an afflicted person with his fan of Eagle feathers. As the feathers gently brush over the person, the *akbaalía* feels the *baaxpée* "pulsate" into the fan through his fingers and arm and then into the patient's body. *Baaxpée* is transferred from "head to foot." The patient feels a "cooling" sensation. With his hand and fan held over the afflicted area, the *akbaalía* feels the "pulse" working. The throbbing continues for a while, and when it begins to cease, the *akbaalía* jerks the fan away from the patient's body, and the ailment is "tossed to the east, letting it blow away." The *baaxpée* has entered the patient's body and removed the illness.

While the "brew" certainly has natural qualities, it also

has transcendent qualities, or *baaxpée*. The Eagle feathers are natural objects, but they are also spiritually endowed. Eagle plumes are mounted on the tips of Eagle-bone whistles, and held by participants as they dance toward the center pole during the Sun Dance. These plumes can be acquired from various sources, but they do not possess *baaxpée* until they have been revealed in and sanctioned by the transcendent. Before such feathers can be brought into the Sun Dance Lodge and used ritually, they must be smudged in sweet grass, which cleanses them, and an *akbaalía* must say prayers over them. This establishes their spiritual significance. They have been brought into a communion with the spiritual, their dual qualities acknowledged.

### Xapáaliia and World View

The "driftwood" world view is expressed in the nature of *xapáaliia*. As a spiritual power, *baaxpée* transcends the material world, emanating from Akbaatatdía, that which is pervasive and omnipotent. As a spiritual power, *baaxpée* manifests itself in the transforming of objects and of lives. It is a guide in life, the wisdom for maturity. It heals the afflicted and, at times, afflicts the healthy. Through the vehicles of *xapáaliia* and the Iilápxe, the ultimate life-force and perennial meaning inherent in the transcendent are channeled forth into the world of the Apsáalooke. The human is interconnected with the transcendent.

CHAPTER 5

# Acquisition of *Xapáaliia:* Fasting

LIKE OTHERS BEFORE HIM, the young man in the story of
the "Yellow Lightning" was in need of help. He was incomplete, like an orphan, and he was seeking completeness,
adoption. The young man's sincerity and sacrifice were rewarded by two gifts of *xapáaliia*, each granted by Akbaatatdía and mediated through an Iilápxe. The young man is no
longer an orphan.

Among the various ways medicine can be acquired, "to
fast from water [and food]" (*bilisshíissanne*) is the most fundamental. Other ways include inheriting a family medicine
bundle or purchasing the "right" to a medicine bundle from
someone who already possesses it.

Whether it takes place during a vision quest, usually
termed a "fast," or during the Sun Dance, fasting is a personal sacrifice. In a vow made before Akbaatatdía, one
pledges to give of himself or herself and to go without food
and water for a prescribed number of days. The act of making
such a vow is termed *baaattaakúuo*. The verb *baaattaakúuo*
also carries the meaning of "desiring a good blessing." Thus
the term implies giving a gift with the hope of receiving
one. The fasting is done on a hill or mountainside, either
alone or in the company of one or two others in the spring,
summer, or fall. It may last from two to as many as four or
five days, although three days is the usual length. If a vision is received before the number of days pledged has
passed, the sacrifice is deemed sufficient, and the faster
may end it. The Sun Dance participant, however, always

77

## YELLOW LIGHTNING

Without letup the June rain poured down throughout the night. But with the arrival of the day's first light the surrounding view is clear, the Wolf Mountains to the east and the Bighorns to the southwest. A young man has come to this high butte to pray and to fast. During the rainy night and on into the two subsequent days and nights yet to come, the private ordeal will continue, the young man seeking a message from Akbaatatdía.

Preparations had been made, and *akbaalía* contacted, a purification sweat bath taken, instructions given, and Iilápxe asked to watch over and aid the young man.

Now naked before all, the faster humbles himself, becoming of no more importance than the smallest of creatures, the ant, who shares this butte with him.

He lights his pipe, pointing its stem toward the morning Sun, and prays. But before the bright disk begins to show itself on the horizon, the first of three visitors arrives. In the path between the rising Sun and the young man, the Eagle makes itself known, soaring from left to right and then flying into the distant eastern hills. It's a sign of a blessing to come.

The presence of the Eagle is followed by that of the Meadowlark, who's come to rest beside the faster. As this Bird has done numerous times for other fasters, it sings a song in Apsáalooke "never heard before." The song, "a good song," is a gift from the Meadowlark to the young man.

The rising of the morning Sun is accompanied by a covering of the yellow-tinted cloud. Within the cloud the young man can clearly see an image of a live Elk. With huge, pronged antlers it moves about, digging into the yellow ground of the cloud. With one antler, then another, the Elk digs into the yellow ground. With each jab, a bit of ground is scattered into the air, falling as if it were yellow paint. As the paint falls, a pattern in the cloud emerges. The *akbaalía* has asked his Fathers to aid the faster, and the Elk has answered. He gives the young man a design which he can paint on himself or on another during a Sun Dance. It's the pattern of "yellow lightning."

The Meadowlark, Baaúuwatshiile

fasts for the three or four days designated for the dance, even if a vision comes earlier.

During the buffalo days, the sacrifice was much more explicit, as "flesh and blood" were literally offered. The famous warrior Two Leggings had horseshoe-shaped pieces of skin removed from his arm by a friend during a fast to help him gain medicine to acquire horses. In 1907, when Lowie first began interviewing Apsáalooke, he found that many of the old people had had a finger joint removed as a sacrifice. Plenty Coups relates how, during one of his fasts,

> I stopped at a fallen tree, and, laying the first finger of my left hand upon the log, I cut part of it off with my knife. . . . But no blood came. The stump of my finger was white as the finger of a dead man, and to make it bleed I struck it against the log until blood flowed freely. Then I began to walk and call for Helpers, hoping that some Person would smell my blood and come aid me. [Linderman 1962:59–60]

Being pierced through the flesh of the breast or back with bone or wooden skewers while one was tied with a stout thong to a pole or buffalo skull was the preferred method of sacrifice. The sacrificer would run about, pulling at the pole or dragging the buffalo head until his skin tore, setting him free. The torn flesh was cut from the body, dried, and offered in prayer as a gift to a spirit Father.

From various accounts of individual fasting and Sun Dancing in both the buffalo days and contemporary times, a recurring pattern emerges. The questing process has a consistent structure involving four distinct yet interdependent components, each of which is essential to the entire process: (1) the orphaned status; (2) the quest; (3) the adoption and the gift of medicine; and (4) the transformation.

## Orphaned Status

Participants fast for various reasons. The verb *bilisshíissannee* literally means "to fast from water" and, by implication, from food as well. A small child, a brother, or an elderly grandmother has become ill; someone is suffering from arthritis, diabetes, or gallstones; a father is paralyzed after a stroke; a child has been listless. All these are reasons why a person may pledge to fast, asking in return for the good health of another.

The reasons for a fast go beyond seeking improvements in health. Thanks is given in the Big Lodge for the recovery of a family member from an affliction; a brother drinks too much, and a wife or child is being abused; a social, economic, or political crisis threatens the stability of the family; a job is needed; children are without proper food and clothing; a young soldier has just left to serve his country in war; indecision haunts a young woman; one has come of age and seeks the guidance and strength needed for maturity. For all these reasons one may dance in the Big Lodge or fast on the hillside.

Whatever prompts an individual to fast, an incompleteness, a lack of ability to cope with a situation, or a state of need characterizes the faster or someone close to him or her. A faster is destitute, alone, in need of help, like an "orphan," *akéeleete*, meaning "one with no possessions, one who has nothing." One of the most commonly used expressions in prayer during a sweat, before a meal, or during a Sun Dance is, "I am poor, pitiful, in need" (*biiwaatcheeshkáatak*). The implication is that the recipient of the prayer should notice the condition of the person praying. As Lowie observed, "No worse insult could be hurled at a Crow than to say, 'You are without relatives'" (Lowie 1983:7).

The incompleteness that motivates a fast need not originate within the faster. "As driftwood lodges," so each individual is an intimate part of his or her family. When one segment of the family is in need, the whole family is in need. Considerable concern is expressed by each member of the family toward the others. If a child or grandmother suffers, a father or granddaughter will offer his or her strength in a fast. As used by the Apsáalooke, the term *baaattaakúuo* also implies a vow to give a gift so that a good blessing will be bestowed on *another* person. In such instances, love for another, not concern for the self, is carried onto the high ridge or into the Big Lodge.

## The Quest

The faster seeks help through a quest into the world of *baaxpée*. "He is looking for something" (*baachichíilik*) is a declarative sentence often used to characterize this situation. By removing oneself from everyday life, one can leave behind one's orphaned status. By sacrificing food and water and offering sincerity, one can gain the aid of an Iilápxe.

A person contemplating a fast may initially seek out an *akbaalía*, telling of the need. Next a sweat bath is taken to purify the quester and to offer prayer that makes one's intentions known to Akbaatatdía. The *akbaalía* may give instructions in the use of the pipe, the Eagle feathers and the cedar that is to be put on the coals of the morning and evening fires. As prayers are given in the sweat, the Iilápxe of the *akbaalía* are asked to watch over the quester.

Physically and spiritually, the faster separates himself or herself from mundane human society. He or she is removed from normal existence to allow entry into the transcendent.

A place for fasting, the Castle Rocks, south of Pryor.

The site of the fast is remote, far from where people normally travel. At the site, the quester may erect a rock wall two or three feet high as a windbreak for the morning and evening fires. The wall is also designed so that passersby cannot see the fire and, becoming curious, decide to investigate. The faster places sweet "man-sage" cuttings around and under his or her bed. Besides warding off dangerous influences, such as "ghosts," the sage is a spiritual garment for a worldly body. Also known as sweet sage, "man sage" is an annual plant frequently used as a spiritual-cleansing and protective agent. The sweat bath has "cleansed you from the inside out," giving spiritual renewal and consecration in addition to physical cleanliness. The faster has abandoned his or her individuality, leaving behind an identity as defined by the world of human beings, an identity that, while one is questing, is no longer important.

During the quest the notion of sacrifice predominates. Offering a gift of value is the necessary first step toward an exchange with the Iilápxe. Besides the outward offering of one's flesh and body by "drying up" and going without food and water, the most cherished gift involves *díakaashe*. Literally meaning "he really did it," the verb *díakaashe* is often loosely translated as "doing it with sincerity, pride, and determination." This inner disposition is revered by the Apsáalooke and the Iilápxe alike. It is the hallmark of one who receives *baaxpée*. On the hill or in the Sun Dance lodge not only the body but also the sincerity of the quester becomes a consecrated offering.

## Adoption and Gift of Xapáaliia

If the quester's gift is deemed worthy, a Father takes pity on him or her, and an exchange is made. Through this exchange the quester participates in the world of *baaxpée*. By offering his or her spiritual essence, the quester is received into a union with Akbaatatdía and receives a vision.

Although the individual enters both the vision quest and the Sun Dance in a consecrated state, the vision experience involves a further level of transcendence. While fasting, the individual becomes a worthy offering for Akbaatatdía, offering what is most vital, offering *díakaashe*. A structural relationship is presupposed involving an exchange between the two acting agents, the faster and Akbaatatdía, a giver and a receiver. Thus one must necessarily be distinct from Akbaatatdía and emphasize within oneself those unique attributes and qualities that are embodied in the act of *díakaashe*. In a vision, however, the faster becomes *baaxpée*. Only by becoming part of Akbaatatdía and merging one's distinctiveness with It, can one receive Its message. The faster addresses the Iilápxe and carries on a dialogue with the spiritual. The fasting state is one of separation from the Maker, while the vision state unites the faster with the Maker. The fasting state involves a quest and a movement toward the transcendent; the vision state involves realization within the transcendent.

## TRANSCENDENT TIME

There's a chill in the air and in the anticipation of what's about to occur. The dancers are lined up in front of and beside the center pole. Pendletons drape their shoulders and Eagle-bone whistles are ready. Just outside the Big Lodge a tape recorder is turned on as the singers begin the morning song. Toward the east the light is growing. Whistles blow to the drumbeat and to the growth of the Sun's light. None stand between those within and that which is about to emerge. Then, as the Sun's rays pierce the eastern horizon, the steady cry of the Eagle's whistle is heard and the beat of the drum picks up. Whistles again blow in unison with the beat and eyes gaze into the Sun. None look away. Some "see something," an animal perhaps, a gift from the Sun. As the bright disk is now complete and the day has begun, the song ends. The tape recorder is turned off. The sunrise song of the Sun Dance is "captured."

Two weeks pass, and the taped song is played before one who "blew the whistle." As the recording draws on, the dancer responds. "They started too early; the song is much too long."

While a person is in the Big Lodge gazing into the Sun or "dancing alongside" the Eagle, or while on a butte when the Elk shows itself, time is suspended. What may last twenty minutes is but a moment during a vision. When the dancer in "Transcendent Time" tried to apply ordinary time to a transcendent moment, an incongruity arose. The duration he remembered and had experienced was qualitatively different from that which was tape-recorded. His comment that "they started too early" reveals his sense that the song now seems long when it had taken only a moment during the Sun Dance. During a vision the normal conventions of time and space are dissolved, and one enters into the undifferentiated, transcendent unity.

The vision establishes a father-child dyad between the quester and the Iilápxe. The Father stands by the quester as a guide. Sometimes a medicine helper may stand within the quester as part of his or her newly expanded essence. One *akbaalía* was adopted by the Elk, which had been the Father of another *akbaalía*, who was "retiring."

While most elements of Apsáalooke religious practice are shared by other Plains Indians, the adoption element and the Father-child relationship seem to be unique to the Apsáalooke (Benedict 1923:16).

In the Iilápxe relationships, the Father, not the child, "owns" the medicine. The Father decides who is "doing it with sincerity and determination" and is thus deserving of the medicine gift. When an *akbaalía* is about to "retire," being too old to carry on his responsibilities, many younger men will seek his power. "I'm the best, I'm worthy, give me your medicine things," they say. But such requests are ignored; the Iilápxe of the "retiring" *akbaalía* decides who will receive the *xapáaliia*. Human beings are only the "caretakers," the "human representatives on earth," of the medicine. They do not "own" it. They are the instruments through which it is applied, but they are not its source. On the death of an elderly *akbaalía*, a bundle may be kept within the family and passed on to a son or daughter for

## THE ELK'S BUGLE

An old friend is up for a winter stay. During the day, after the grandkids are off to school and all the chores are done, it's a good time to visit, a time to talk about the medicine things. The old man is passing on his medicine to this younger man, a man who has not sought it, but who has been chosen to receive it. One day, a tape recorder is turned on and the songs sung by the old man are captured. It's a good way to learn the songs. The tapes can be played over and over again until the songs are learned. Each day something of the medicine things is talked about. Toward the end of his stay, the old man says it's time for a little ceremony. It's evening. Everyone is fed. The grandkids are told to sit still on the living-room couches. The overhead lights are turned down. A bundle is opened and its objects carefully smudged with sweet grass incense and placed at the center of the floor. After prayer is given, the old man instructs his friend to stand and face the east. The old man stands right behind. A small pipe stem is pressed against the back and blown by the old man. As the breath travels through the stem, the bugle of the Elk is heard just outside, startling the grandkids, and the Elk enters the body of this *akbaalía*. He will always be on hand to advise and aid as a father does. The Elk remains in the chest of the man, a man chosen by the Elk.

## A PLEDGE FULFILLED

It's the last evening of a three-day fast. A huge cloud covers the Sun as it falls below the horizon. As a young man watches it, the vivid image of an Eagle is revealed. One after another, three distinct views of the Eagle are seen. He gives thanks.

During the previous days he has lit a fire to the rising and setting Sun, offering a sweet cedar smudging and a prayer with the pipe. Each day, as it becomes hot, the faster walks the path to a high ridge not far from his sage-flanked bedding. The path takes him past a rattlesnake den. Without fear, he sits down a few feet from the coiled body of a small rattler, the same one who greets him each day. To do so but a few days ago would have been unthinkable. But during the fast, relationships change, or perhaps, they become clearer. After a brief conversation, the man continues his short journey to the ridge. Under the Sun's watch, thoughts of his family, and particularly his son, concern him. His son has suffered, has been ill, and as a consequence, the man and his entire family suffered. A pledge has been made; a gift will be given if a small boy recovers. The boy has regained his health and now on this hill a pledge is being fulfilled.

While the sky holds only a sliver of a moon, the stars are bright. In the calm of the night air, an uneasiness overcomes the faster. He becomes anxious, his palms sweating, his heart beating loudly. A cigarette is lit and prayer is given. What he fears, he's not sure, but halfway into the third cigarette a visitor appears. Up from the south slope and not more than five feet away, stands one of the Little People. Without speaking or motioning, the presence brings a calm back to the night air and to the faster. And as it does the Dwarf is gone, and a deep sleep falls over the young man.

It must be close to noon when he decides it's time to come down off the hill. His pledge is fulfilled; the gift given his son is reciprocated. But he knows that he has not accomplished it alone. The prayers of an old man, an *akbaalía*, had been shared in a sweat before the fast, and then given again each day while the young man fasted on the hill. The Iilápxe had been asked to watch over a "grandson," and they had; the Eagle and Dwarf were close at hand.

safekeeping. In this case, the *xapáaliia* might not be used
unless the Iilápxe designated that it could be. A bundle also
may simply be weighted down with rocks and thrown into
the river along with a prayer.

## Transformation

When a quester completes a fast, the acquired medicine
gives a completeness to his or her orphaned existence; a
transformation has occurred, either in the faster or in another. Perhaps someone's illness has been cured, a family
crisis has been met successfully, thanks have been received,
guidance has been offered, or a powerful essence has been
added to the character of the faster through a vision. Someone has been adopted by the Iilápxe. For what has been
offered in the act of *díakaashe*, the faster returns as a new
self, a transformed being. Thus through the offering of one's
sincerity and determination, the transcendent can be realized within oneself or within another.

A quester may take a sweat upon his or her return. At
that time he or she relates to the *akbaalía* who aided in the
quest whatever vision came to him or her during the fast.
The *akbaalía* offers an interpretation of the spiritual experience along with additional instructions for the care that
should be given the *xapáaliia*.

## Oral Literature and Ritual Behavior

The four components of the quest, central to the rituals
of fasting and Sun Dancing, are replicated in traditional
Apsáalooke oral literature. Second in popularity to the
trickster-hero stories of Old Man Coyote are "tales of supernatural patrons" (Lowie 1918). Typical are stories such as
that of the poor boy who, while fasting, is adopted by the
Sun and instructed in the creation of the Tobacco Society.
Clara Ehrlich has broadly defined three recurring aspects
of these tales: the vision quest, the supernatural adoption,
and the demonstration of spiritual power (1939:402). To
these three, our initial aspect, orphaned status, can be
added. In "tales of supernatural patrons" the quest is al-

most always predicated on a need to overcome some handicap. Even if not expressly stated, an orphaned status of some kind is the implicit motivation for the quest. In the last of the four structural components—the demonstration of spiritual power—transformation of the human occurs. A significant portion of the oral literature thus structurally replicates the four components of the quest: the orphaned status, the quest, the adoption and the acquisition of medicine, and the transformation.

The story of Burnt Face, which is still heard today, exemplifies the four-part structure of Apsáalooke oral literature. Because of his disfigurement, Burnt Face is symbolic of an orphan—incomplete and unable to reach the highly regarded ideal of manhood, physical bodily perfection. He is scarred for life.

Oral literature has an immediate and personal influence on the lives of the Apsáalooke. Two Leggings, a buffalo-day warrior, readily maintained that his life and his self-image were patterned after those of Bear White Child (Nabokov 1967:6–10). Paralleling the story of Burnt Face, the tale of Bear White Child involves a young boy, orphaned and abused by an adversary, who is adopted by a powerful spirit helper, Bear Up-above, and overcomes his opponent to gain recognition and success. Two Leggings saw himself as handicapped and alone, and throughout his life he attempted to gain the spirit Father who, in turn, would help him overcome his suffering and achieve his rightful status.

Similarly, it is not uncommon, when someone is attempting to convey a specific event or a peculiar trait in another's personality, to begin the characterization with an abbreviated version of an Old Man Coyote story. It is as if the story is used not only as a guide for better understanding of the characterization but also as the model for the original event or idiosyncracy. As one young Apsáalooke man said, "We just don't enjoy listening to Old Man Coyote stories, we enjoy acting them out." While interviewing Yellow-brow in 1931, Lowie was told, regarding sexual activity, that with the exception of a virtuous woman "one followed one's natu-

## BURNT FACE

It's dusk and a young boy is running through camp. He must be chasing another. As he runs, and not particularly watchful, he stumbles and falls into a fire pit. The hot coals burn the right side of his face badly. His mother hears his cries and is quickly at his side. Prairie-dog-tail (yarrow) is chewed and placed with care on the burn. After he's brought back to his lodge, an old man offers prayer over him. The pain is gone but a bad scar remains. Over the next couple of years, the face becomes an object of ridicule and shame.

"Look, there he is, there's Burnt Face; he's bad to look at."

Seldom does he come out of his lodge, and then only with his face painted over. But still they know, and tears come to the eyes of Burnt Face. He hates part of himself.

No longer a boy, Burnt Face tells his mother to make him some moccasins. She's reluctant at first, but she makes them, knowing what her son must do. Burnt Face goes alone into the hills to the south. Holes come to his moccasins and another pair is put on. Higher he goes until he is in the Bighorns. There above the trees, where the Sun rises and sets unobstructed, where the wind constantly blows, Burnt Face begins his fast. During the day he spends his time moving large stones to form a great circle, a "medicine wheel." It can still be seen there, high in the mountains.* He gives of himself so that he might receive something.

One day, as he looks out toward the east, he sees an odd sight. There among the trees is a wind, a twister. As it moves closer, it becomes stronger; lodgepole pines break at their trunks as if they were twigs. It moves closer and with pipe in hand, Burnt Face waits. Just as it is about to blow him off the knoll, the twister stops. Where there had been wind, there stands a great Eagle.

*The "medicine wheel" credited to Burnt Face is also thought by others to have been assembled by Áxxaashe, the Sun. Lowie mentions that the site was frequented not only by Apsáalooke fasters but also by the Sun, a place of the "Sun's lodge." According to Flat-Dog, one of Lowie's informants, the circle of stone was "a lodge made for the Sun and used by him as a camping-place" (1922c: 436). Robert Hall, in a comparative study of medicine wheels, suggests that much of the symbolic significance of the Bighorn medicine wheel is that of a "world center shrine," through which communications with, and the powers of, Sky, Earth, and Spirit are channeled to humans (1985:181–93). In 1903, S. C. Simms described the medicine wheel as a circle about 245 feet in diameter, with a "hub" 3 feet high and 27 "spokes," all made of stone (1903b:108–109).

"Why are you crying, my son, why are you crying?"

"Because I hate part of myself; I'm bad to look at."

"If you help me, I'll help you, my son."

Burnt Face gets on the back of the huge Bird and they fly to the south. Upon landing, Burnt Face goes into a small lodge and finds two small Eagles.

"Why are you crying, my brother, why are you crying?"

"Because I hate part of myself; I'm bad to look at."

"Go make me a bow and set of arrows."

"Go make me a ball and stick so I can play shinny."

With the finest of materials and with care, Burnt Face makes these things for the children of the Eagle.

"Why are you crying, my brother, why are you crying?"

"I hate part of myself; I'm bad to look at."

One of the Eagles goes to the liner of the lodge and pulls out a mirror. Holding it up, Burnt Face looks into it. What he sees is a new face and tears come to his eyes. He's like a newborn child. And then the great Eagle comes in.

"Over that ridge there is a fast-moving river. In it lives the Long Otter. We're not safe because of the Otter. You must help us."

Burnt Face crosses over the ridge and as he does picks up dry wood and four stones, like those used in a sweat. On the river-bank a fire is lit and the rocks are heated up. Burnt Face waits. Suddenly it becomes still and a fog moves out from the water. But then it is as it was. A second time a thick fog covers the land and the birds no longer can be heard. But it is soon gone. A third time the fog and the stillness roll in. But as before, as quickly as it came, it's gone. More wood is put on the fire. Then a fourth time a fog, much thicker than before, covers the land in darkness. It's midday, but it's like night. A short moment before, the wind had stirred the leaves in the trees. But now all is quiet. In the still-ness a faint sound is heard. It's getting louder; it's moving toward Burnt Face. Suddenly the outstretched jaws of the Long Otter greet Burnt Face. He immediately picks up the glowing rocks. One, two, then a third and the fourth are thrown into the mouth that hungers for something else. The Long Otter rolls this way, then that, and then back into the fast-moving waters. As he goes, the sun and the song of the birds return. The Eagle stands beside Burnt Face.

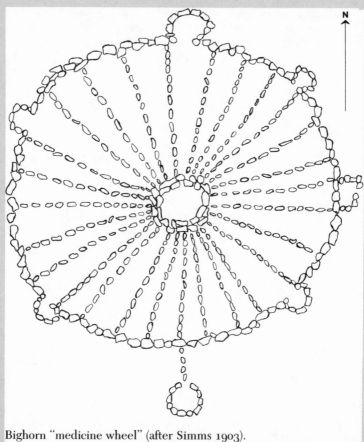

N
↑

Bighorn "medicine wheel" (after Simms 1903).

"I shall be with you always, as a father is with his son. Paint on your lodge my picture and wear about your neck my claws."

Burnt Face marries and lives to such a great age that when he moves his skin tears. That's old!*

*With the exception of the addition of the "medicine wheel" reference, this informant's account of Burnt Face closely parallels the one recorded by Lowie (1918:152–56).

ral bent for pleasure according to Old Man Coyote's example" (1983:47).

The relevance of oral literature to the lives of the Apsáalooke can also be seen in the instance of Mike. Mike is a
prominent *akbaalía* who "runs" Sun Dances each summer
and uses his gifts to help those in need. In the Big Lodge
he is a giving, family-focused man, thinking about concerns
other than himself. He is a steadfastly honest man and would
never deliberately treat another person unfairly. As a generous, giving person, as *bachéem*, Mike has never "charged
a fee" for his doctoring services. He has a reputation as one
who has never publicly become angry with another person.
In the context of the Sun Dance religion, Mike follows the
path of the Eagle and Burnt Face, seeking to strengthen
the interdependence of the kinship ties around him.

While the imagery of Burnt Face and the Eagle characterizes much of Mike's behavior, occasionally another image arises. One afternoon during Crow Fair, Mike decided
to take in the rodeo and horse races. Unfortunately he was
short of money, but that did not stop him. Without hesitation he marched to the front of a long line of people waiting
to enter the arena grandstands as if he were a rodeo official
and needed to get in. The gatekeeper immediately and
without question allowed the "official" in. When Mike returned home that evening, he delighted in talking not about
the rodeo but about his trick.

That afternoon Mike had used deception to gain an advantage for himself. He had played the part of Old Man Coyote,
who in most situations is an assertive, self-gratifying trickster. Mike consciously manipulated his immediate world
for his own advantage.

There is thus a close interchange between oral literature
and human activity. The Apsáalooke are equally comfort-
able in either realm. Indeed, in their daily lives they often
become the characters and act out the events from their
oral traditions.

## OLD MAN COYOTE AND THE WHIRLWIND

It's Old Man Coyote. There's a beautiful woman whom everyone wants to marry. But once they do, no one can stay married for long. Old Man Coyote desires this woman very much, and says he can stay married to her. He tells her he wants to marry her. "I'm the best looking man around, and most intelligent too. You couldn't find a better man than me!" This sounds pretty good to the woman. So they get married and Old Man Coyote is satisfied.

After a while the woman says, "I'll move camp." When it gets dark, she takes down the lodge and ties up all her things. She makes Old Man Coyote sit beside her on the bundle, and they fly off. She's the Whirlwind, a witch. Traveling all night, they set up camp in the morning and sleep all day. Her days are her nights. When the Sun goes down, she moves camp again. In the morning, she sets up the lodge and cooks a meal for Old Man Coyote. She sleeps during the day and travels at night. And that's the way it goes.

Well, this isn't what Old Man Coyote had bargained for. He's having a pretty difficult time of it. He tries to sleep at night while they travel, but just can't. And during the day when he's awake, his wife is asleep. What kind of marriage is that? Old Man Coyote is exhausted. So he thinks it over and gets an idea.

That day Old Man Coyote tells Whirlwind he's going hunting and will be gone all day. He's off. But he knows she'll be after him. So he changes himself into a mouse and hides out in a mouse lodge.

After a while, Whirlwind comes to the lodge. "I'm looking for my husband; have you seen him?" "Well, who is he?" the mouse says; the mouse is really Old Man Coyote. "He's my husband, that's all I know." "Oh, yes, he's no good. He's the one who goes around tricking everybody. No good," the mouse tells her. "If I had known that, I'd never marry him." And Whirlwind leaves.

Old Man Coyote returns as he was before. He thought he could have any woman he desired, but he met his match. He goes off, tricking those he comes across but stays away from Whirlwind.*

*This story was shared by a participant and was also recorded by Lowie along with an entire series of Old Man Coyote stories (1918:14–51). As with all Old Man Coyote stories the Whirlwind story should only be told aloud during the winter, between the first frost and the first thunder.

## Unsolicited Baaxpée

While the explicit motivation for fasting is nearly always a specific need, usually related to a crisis in one's family, the underlying desire is that a medicine will be bestowed on the faster. Implicit in the fast and the Sun Dance is the quest for, the solicitation of, *xapáaliia*. Many times, however, medicine is acquired unsolicited. When a prominent *akbaalía* is about to "retire," someone must be chosen by the Fathers to carry on the benefits of the *baaxpée*. If an individual has shown integrity, has been *díakaashe*, *xapáaliia* may be given, even when it has not been sought. On several occasions, the natural son of an *akbaalía* has been the recipient of *xapáaliia* even though he had not anticipated such a gift. On these occasions the father-child dyad is expressed on both a spiritual and a social plane.

Even when a gift of medicine has not been received through a vision, *baaxpée* still resides in the *xapáaliia*. The Iilápxe may convey to their new son or daughter the specific intentions and responsibilities associated with the subsequent application of the medicine. Dreams eventually will be sent. During future fasts the son or daughter will share in their spiritual power by participating in a dialogue with the Iilápxe.

No matter what the particulars of its bestowal, whether it is given on a hill, in the Sun Dance lodge, or whether it is unsolicited, the gift of medicine always remedies an incompleteness. The recipient is no longer an orphan.

## Xapáaliia and World View

The "driftwood" world view is expressed in the acquisition of *xapáaliia*. Many aspects of Apsáalooke oral literature and ritual are overt reminders of the need for a firm lodging in the driftwood. Without such placement, one is *akéeleete*, an orphan. To receive that which can heal, resolve an indecision, or bring completeness, a sacrifice must be given. In offering oneself, being sincere, and "drying up," the orphan is "adopted," and union with the transcendent is real-

## THE TWO FEATHERS

During a warm summer night, a man has a dream of an event that's yet to occur. In his vision he sees an adult Eagle sitting on a hillside. A man he knows well, a clan brother, approaches the Bird and proceeds to pull out two tail feathers, the evenly matched pair of the twelve tail feathers, while the Eagle simply looks on. After the man has completed his task, the Eagle flies off.

Soon after, the dream is retold to an *akbaalía*, and only to the *akbaalía*.

Some time has passed, and the man seen in the dream is alone, driving back from Billings. On a small bluff, not far from the road, the man sees a large Eagle perched on a rock outcropping. Stopping the car instantly, he walks up to the Bird. It doesn't attempt to fly away, but quietly watches the man as he pulls the two feathers from his tail. The Bird then flies off.

Not knowing what to make of the event, the man takes the feathers to an *akbaalía* and asks what should be done with them. The *akbaalía* relates the dream and tells the man "these feathers are meant to be yours." The *akbaalía* keeps the feathers for a few days, "making medicine" of them, smudging them over a fire and giving prayer. That which was not sought but needed is bestowed on a young man.

ized within the self. The Eagle becomes an Iilápxe and watches over a "son" or "daughter." The wisdom for maturity is imparted. To maintain the "adoption," one must continue to respect and care properly for the *xapáaliia*. In so doing, the "son" or "daughter" is molded by the *xapáaliia;* the human is interconnected with the transcendent.

# CHAPTER 6

# Acquisition of *Xapáaliia:*
# Sun Dance

THE SUN DANCE (Ashkísshe) is structurally similar to the ritual of the vision quest. In both instances, *baaattaakúuo*, the making of a private vow to Akbaatatdía, precedes participation. The vow expresses the needs of an orphaned individual. Fasting (*bilisshíissannee*) is the means of sacrifice in both rituals, and if an individual is sincere (*díakaashe*), a vision and adoption by the Iilápxe may transpire. The ritual processes for both the Sun Dance and the fast focus on the individual's sacrifice and spiritual attainment.

While the fast is entirely an individual and private endeavor, however, the Sun Dance is an aggregate of individual expressions, dramatically demonstrating concern and love for family, tribe, and humanity. Ties with family and friends are reaffirmed and strengthened. A lodge is built, cattails are collected and given out, songs are sung, and a feast is prepared and served, all to those who offer their prayers and themselves in the Sun Dance. The prayers offered during the Sunrise ceremony may be directed at the welfare of a family member, of an entire family, of all the Apsáalooke, or of all people. During the Sun Dance, an *akbaalía* stands before the center pole, using his Eagle feathers to "touch up" and doctor a child being held by its mother. Charging the center pole and blowing his Eagle-bone whistle to the beat of the drum, a father "dries up" so that his son, looking on at the lodge door, will grow strong. And the rising smoke of a cigarette held by a participant stand-

An elder dancing in the Big Lodge.

ing in front of the same pole carries a prayer for the grand-mother sitting just outside the Sun Dance lodge.

### Preparations

The preparations for a Sun Dance are extensive and have become more so in recent years, with two and occasionally three Sun Dances being held on the reservation each summer. First, a sponsor for the dance comes forward after having vowed (*baaattaakúuo*) to "put up" a dance. Like the vows of all who will accompany him into the Big Lodge, the sponsor's vow reflects some kind of incompleteness. The public announcement to sponsor a Sun Dance usually occurs at the conclusion of one Sun Dance or at a prayer meeting held sometime during the winter before the dance is to take place. At this time the sponsor asks an *akbaalía* to "run" the dance for him. Only certain individuals have been given the "authority" to coordinate and officiate over such a ceremony. This authority is granted by those who will dance and by an *akbaalía* who once had the "authority" and has passed it on. Also during the public announcement the site at which the dance will be held and the specific dates for it, usually a weekend in late June or July, are conveyed. The news of a forthcoming Sun Dance soon becomes known to those who may desire to "blow the whistle." Among those who will be offering a vow are women. They have participated as dancers in the Sun Dance since the 1950s, although they have not acted as sponsors or *akbaalía* of the ceremony.

Usually after the *suuwassée* (the first spring thunder), a ceremony is held at the site where the Sun Dance will take place. A fire is made, sweet cedar is burned, and a prayer is offered to Isáahka, the "Old Man," telling Him where the center pole of the lodge will be placed. A stake is then driven into the ground to mark the spot. A wooden mallet must be used to drive the stake in, and it must be swung only three times. For every extra hit and for every missed hit an extra day must be added to the dance. As a precaution the mallet used is quite large, having approximately an eight-inch head.

The prayer and the marking ceremony are considered the first of four "outdoor dances" held at the site. These "rehearsal dances," as they are also known, are attended by the sponsor, the *akbaalía*, and a group of singers, while a score of others looks on, many of whom will dance in the Sun Dance. Songs are sung, and the sponsor and the *akbaalía*, dressed as they will be in the Big Lodge, blow their Eagle-bone whistles and "charge" and dance back away from a fire about twenty feet in front of them. A feast is offered at the conclusion of each rehearsal dance. The remaining three dances are often held on the evenings immediately preceding the start of the actual Sun Dance ceremony, with the fourth, and final, rehearsal dance held the night before the ceremony starts.

Also in the spring, before the budding of the trees, the *balasáhte* (forked tree) is selected. At that time of year a "clearer view" of the trees' branches is available. Also called the "center pole," the *balasáhte* is a two-pronged tree, thirty to fifty feet high. A straight, sturdy tree, usually cottonwood, is sought. Pine, because it can split more easily under the weight of the twelve overhead poles and cause "bad luck," is seldom used. The *balasáhte* is located, but it is not cut until just before the three-day Sun Dance ceremony.

With rehearsal dances occurring during the evenings, the days immediately preceding the dance are set aside for the cutting and gathering of the poles and rafters needed for constructing the lodge. The sponsor and his family are responsible for these preparations. The center pole is usually cut on the morning of the day the Sun Dance begins. The sponsor, the *akbaalía*, and a host of young men gather around the forked tree. The *akbaalía* offers a prayer. Holding a lit pipe with the stem pointed to the top of the tree, the *akbaalía* tells the tree of its forthcoming role and requests its assistance. Four successive bursts of an Eagle-bone whistle signal the end of the prayer. An Eagle-feather fan, smudged in the incense of burning sweet grass, is used to "touch up" the great tree. An individual of undisputed honor and great deeds, perhaps a veteran of a foreign war, strikes the base of the tree several times with an ax, "counting coup" on it. The tree is then cut. After the tree hits the ground, the observers look for sap running from the stump. If observed, this is a "good sign," and one after another, with the sponsor and the *akbaalía* going first, all who are present collect sap in their hands and rub the "tree's life" onto their chests and heads. A blessing is received. The forked tree is shorn of its branches and taken by truck to the site of the dance.

At dawn on the morning on which the center pole is to be raised into place, a "line up" is made at the dance site. The spot where the *akbaalía*, the "chief," will sit is aligned with the morning Sun just as it appears on the horizon. That spot will be linked to the center pole by the "chief pole," one of the twelve overhead rafters. Also in line with the Sun, and directly east of the stake marking the center pole's place, the entrance of the lodge is marked.

With the "line up" marked and the forked tree cut and brought to the dance site, the Big Lodge (Ashé Isée) can be erected. The first step is to raise the center pole. A hole four feet deep is dug where the pole will go. An honored soldier who has returned from military service "without a scratch" tells "his story" to those gathered. Relayed through the voice of an "announcer" or the *akbaalía*, the veteran relates a "close call" and asks that the "good fortune" that was his now be with the dancers. With the ashes and charcoals from the fire of the previous evening's rehearsal dance mixed in a can of water, the veteran marks three charcoal bands on the pole. Each band represents one of the days of the Sun Dance. Occasionally four rings are marked, signifying a four-day dance. In the past twelve years, two four-day Sun Dances have been held. Two flags, one blue and the other white, having been donated by a family, are tied, along with a bag of Bull Durham tobacco, just below the

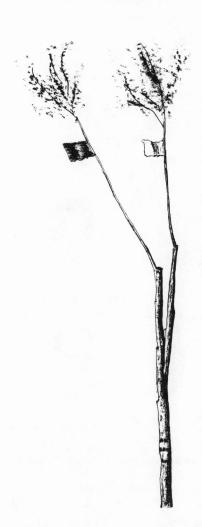

The center pole just after being placed back in the Earth.

Tom Yellowtail with the Sun Dance sponsor just before the Buffalo is placed on the center pole.

leaves on the two branches of the tree. The blue flag flies to the north; the white to the south. While some say these flags represent the cycle of day and night, the blue for the night and the white for the day, others hold that they symbolize the continuity of the universe, with blue for the heavens and white for the earth. White has the additional meaning of "purity and truth." As the "song of the tree" is sung by all those gathered, perhaps thirty to forty individuals, the tree is lifted horizontally from the ground and then gently lowered back down. The song and the horizontal lifting of the tree are repeated four times. On the fourth, the center pole, with guide ropes attached, is raised into position with its base in the hole. The forked tree is thus reunited with the Earth. The crotch is positioned so that it opens to the east, toward the rising Sun.

Various families donate twelve smaller forked cottonwood posts. They give these in anticipation of receiving a gift from Akbaatatdía. A circle is marked on the ground around and away from the center pole. Around the perimeter of this circle holes are dug for the twelve smaller posts. The one that will be attached to the "chief pole" goes west of the center pole, five go to the north, and six to the south, all evenly spaced. After these posts are erected, twelve lodgepole pine rafters, beginning with the "chief pole," are lifted and joined to the center pole from the smaller forked posts. The "chief pole" is also chosen for its forked tip, and at its cutting it is given a prayer, telling it of its duties and asking for its assistance.

The overhead poles may be as long as "sixteen paces," or approximately thirty-six to forty feet. The lodge must be big enough to accommodate a large number of dancers. Since 1974, from 85 to 120 dancers have participated in each Sun Dance. In 1975, the Big Lodge (located between Wyola and Lodge Grass), as large as any lodge ever built, had to be extended to house unexpected additional dancers. After the overhead poles are in place, the lodge is enclosed on all sides but the east with pine trees or cottonwood brush. The east side is left open to greet the fasters and the morning Sun.

The center pole is given its final form when the head of a Buffalo, a mounted Eagle, and a bundle of Willows are attached near the fork. The Little Old Man, one of the Little People and the "big chief" who "owns" the lodge, is already at his watch, and the Big Lodge is ready to receive the questers.

## ASKING FOR GOOD FORTUNE

The late morning Sun is hot, approaching ninety degrees. Some forty men, including several non-Indians, are gathered close by the center pole. It lays there, forks to the west and base near the four foot hole. The flags and tobacco have just been attached and the tree is ready for the charcoal bands. A man in his late thirties steps forward and speaks to an "announcer." The older man, with head lowered, periodically nods at what's being told to him. After a few minutes, the veteran steps back and, with a clear and loud voice, the "announcer" relates to those gathered what had been shared with him.

"This young man's on patrol in Vietnam, on a reconnaissance mission, searching out the enemy. He finds himself alone in a great field and senses he's being watched. The enemy is close at hand and he's scared. He knows he's an easy target. But he continues on his mission and, with Akbaatatdía with him, walks out of that field without a scratch. This field here, where we're putting up this lodge, reminds him of that field in Vietnam. He's asking that the good fortune that was his in Vietnam be here with the Sun Dance and all those who will be using the whistle."

The coffee can of charcoal mixed in water is set beside the center pole and the veteran steps forward again, along with his son. Guiding the boy's hand, the father paints the first band around the pole. The veteran then completes the task alone, placing two more charcoal bands around the forked tree. Three bands, each painted with care by one who had "good fortune," mark the three days of the Sun Dance.

It's a Sun Dance that indeed brings much "good fortune."

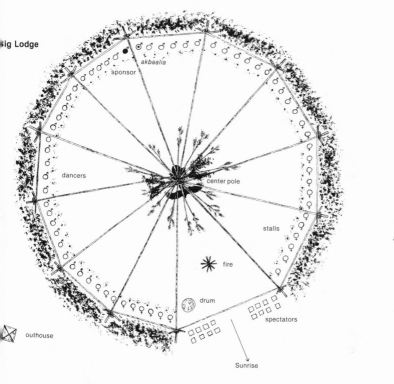

The Big Lodge.

The center pole provides the medium of communication between the Sun Dance participants and Akbaatatdía. As the twelve overhead poles point to and depend on the center pole for support, so the dancers focus and depend on it in their prayers, their "charges," and their quest for a cure and a vision. The Buffalo head, facing west with sweet "man-sage" bundles tied close to its nostrils, offers its essence, the meat of life. The Willows, which grow near the flowing waters of the land, offer the liquid of life as they hang in a large bundle on the east side of the tree just be-

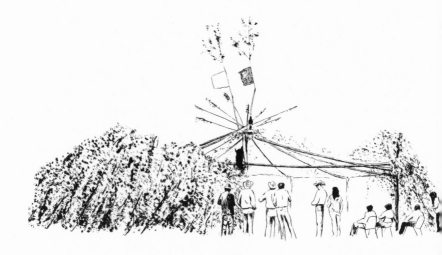

The Sun Dance Lodge, Ashé Isée.

low the crotch. The Eagle, with its unrivaled strength and beauty, soars above all, secured atop the "chief pole."

In the context of the Sun Dance religion the Eagle "touches" the participants from "head to foot" as the *ak-baalía* "works on" them with his feathers. While participants dance in the Big Lodge, the cry of the Eagle is heard from the whistles. Made from the wing bone of the Eagle, the plumed whistles are blown in unison to the beat of the drum. As the dancers charge the center pole, their attention may be focused on the Eagle suspended from the pole. The Eagle may accompany a dancer in the sought-after vision, dancing alongside and instructing him (it is usually men who receive visions during the dance) in the ways of the newly acquired medicine. On the second day of the dance, a dancer may see the Eagle soaring high above the Big Lodge. The Eagle is alive with a beauty and strength unmatched anywhere, having been endowed with keen eyesight as well as foresight. The Eagle's appearance stimulates excitement. It carries the Maker's messages and is a symbol of a blessing to come.

The center pole is imbued with the qualities of the Buffalo, the Willow, and the Eagle. The rays of the morning Sun are captured between its two forks, which tower open to the sky, to Akbaatatdía, while its roots are anchored in the Earth. Thus the center pole allows the dialogue needed for a vision, for a cure, or for an answer to a prayer. It is a channel to Akbaatatdía, through which *baaxpée* flows.[1]

Throughout the dance, in addition to the support offered by the lodge and the center pole, the families and friends of the dancers will be present outside the lodge to offer assistance and encouragement. They will be camped on all sides of the lodge except the east and will stay far enough away so that the smells of their morning and evening cooking cannot be detected by the fasters (theoretically, at least). Groups of male singers, accompanied by a female chorus, will offer song throughout most of the dance. Seated around a bass drum, the singers will be located just inside the door of the Sun Dance Lodge. When one group tires, having sung continuously for several hours, another group will take its place.

After sunset but before midnight on the day the Big Lodge is completed, the men and women dancers, divided into two groups, one led by the sponsor, the other by the *akbaalia* "running" the Dance, gather near the west side of the lodge. Many have taken a sweat during the afternoon, and all have had a "good meal." All are fully dressed, the men in brightly colored ankle-length skirts and the women in calico dresses, most with elegantly beaded or engraved leather belts, and all barefoot with plumed Eagle-bone whistles hanging from their necks. Each man has a Pendleton blanket folded over his arm, and each woman has one draped over her shoulders. Moving in opposite directions,

[1] For a penetrating and faithful presentation of the symbolism and meaning of the Lakota Sun Dance and other rites and thus, by extension, all Plains Indian ceremonialism, including the Apsáalooke, see Brown (1953).

The Eagle-bone whistle.

the men blowing their whistles in unison, the two groups circle the Big Lodge twice, entering on the second round. The Sun Dance has begun.[2]

### Prayer

The most subtle, yet in many respects the most fundamental, ritual in the Sun Dance ceremony is *chiwakíia*. The verb *chiwakíia* refers to the act of prayer, literally meaning "to ask repeatedly." In prayer one's intentions are stated. In prayer each supplicant reiterates his or her personal vow before Akbaatatdía, stating his or her reasons for giving of himself or herself.

During the first day and evening of the dance, an individual will walk out to the center pole, being careful not to walk between the center pole and another dancer, for nothing should interfere with a dancer's link to the forked tree, the avenue to Akbaatatdía. Holding a lit cigarette aloft, a dancer gives a prayer. While a dancer is alongside the cen-

[2]Voget (1984) and Fitzgerald (forthcoming) offer additional discussion of the rituals connected with erecting the Big Lodge as well as with the Sun Dance ceremony itself.

## A "CLEAR" PATH

For the past several months she's been troubled by the death of her brother. Though his death had been an accident, and she was in no way to blame, she feels a heavy burden of guilt. She's a woman caught between two worlds, the traditional world of her grandmother and the modern world to which her college education and career have led her. It's a conflict between the "Indian way" and the "non-Indian way." Her inability to reconcile the differences between the two and choose a "path" leads her on the eve of the Sun Dance to decide to "go in" and "use the whistle."

She'll not dance too much; fasting in her stall is enough. Standing alone before the center pole with a lit cigarette in her right hand, which is raised toward the top of the tree, she prays. The cry of the Eagle-bone whistles "charging" the center pole, the steady beat of the drum, and high-pitched voices continue all about her. She's now with Akbaatatdía.

At the completion of her prayer the woman gives thanks, *ahóo*, and offers up the remaining tobacco, extinguishing the "smoke" at the base of the center pole in the small mound of earth that surrounds it. She walks back to her stall, rejoining the company of some 115 other dancers.

What she seeks is given; a clear "path" is laid before her.

Standing at the center pole with a lit cigarette, a dancer offers a prayer.

ter pole giving prayer, the song begun by the singers cannot be ended. The song aids the prayer. "As the smoke rises, so may the words of the prayer" ascend to the Maker. A desire for someone's health, a request for a gift, a vow—the prayer is carried forth as the smoke ascends. The cigarette is then extinguished in the mound that surrounds the base of the center pole. By day's end the mound will we completely covered with the butts of offered cigarettes.

On the second day of the dance, relatives of those within the lodge and other individuals not participating stand at the lodge entrance and ask the "announcer" to summon certain dancers. Each dancer is given a pack of cigarettes and asked to pray for a special intention. During the dance, the dancer will offer the prayer that has been requested. By the end of the ceremony many of the dancers will have received as many as thirty packs of cigarettes.

The "smoke," the offering of cigarette tobacco or of kinnikinnick in the pipe, becomes a vehicle on which a message can be sent. It bridges a gap to allow a dialogue. The "smoke," however, can do more than establish dialogue. It can help bring together those hostile toward, and disparate from, each other. It can seal a union, as suggested in the story of "The Offered Cigarette."

In addition to individual prayers, collective prayer is offered. Each morning, just before sunrise, the "announcer" circles the lodge clockwise, periodically calling out to the dancers, singers, and all others who are gathered that it is time to prepare for the new day. Within the lodge the dancers form rows in front of and behind the center pole, all facing the spot where the Sun (Áxxaashe) will rise. The men line up in the middle, flanked on either side by the women. All are barefoot and have their Eagle-bone whistles hanging from their necks. Pendleton blankets drape their shoulders to keep out the chill morning air. Six or so singers gather around the drum, and a dozen or so others remain just outside the lodge on either side of its entrance.

Just before dawn, the Sunrise song begins. Standing in their rows, the dancers blow their whistles to the beat of the drum. But as the steady rhythm of the drum and the

## THE OFFERED CIGARETTE

A fight breaks out in a Hardin bar, and Pete quickly finds himself
outmatched by the two brothers. He's left in a "bad way." But
Pete knows he'll have "his day," and so too does the father of the
brothers; Pete is a former champion Golden Gloves boxer. A
week or so after the incident, the father comes to Pete's home and
without saying a word, simply offers him a cigarette. Pete has to
accept it, and as he does, any thought of "revenge is gone." What
had been apart is apart no longer.

high-pitched voices of the singers continue, it becomes evident that no human agent is responsible for the tempo. The progressive growth of the new day's Sun on the horizon sets the pace. With the first appearance of the Sun's rays over the horizon, the once distinguishable rhythm of the whistles becomes the steady cry of the Eagle, the sound flowing into the eastern brilliance. As the Sun becomes fuller, the song becomes more intense. Whistles blow harder, and singers sing with increasing fervor.

All eyes stare straight into the Sun. Faces and bodies become clothed in its rays. None look away. None are hurt by its brilliance. The path between the Sun and the dancers is direct, and no one can interrupt the prayer. To cross the path of the Sunlight would be to interfere with the communication, and misfortune might follow anyone who dared. Specially designated men watch and warn any who wander into the path.

As with the "smoke," the song becomes a bridge between the dancers and the rising Sun, spiritually uniting all. Each person merges his or her identity with the totality of the moment. Many are given the gift of seeing a vision in the Sun.

The Sunrise song lasts for ten to fifteen minutes. When it ends, the women return to their places around the inner wall of the lodge. The men remain, seated east of the center pole near the coals and ashes of the fire, which was kept burning throughout the night. With their Pendletons wrapped around their shoulders, the men face the morning Sun and begin another song. This time, however, the drum and the other singers remain quiet. The men sing four songs, each separated by the sound of the Eagle, made as the whistles blow. The *akbaalía* then stands and sprinkles sweet cedar, taken from a small pouch, over the hot coals. A prayer is given. The *akbaalía* asks that what is being sought by the dancers be received, that they have the "will power" to continue with sincerity. The *akbaalía* also seeks the well-being of all the Apsáalooke, of all Indian peoples, and, in fact, of all peoples. Concerns for those close to

home as well as for those across the oceans are thus heard
in prayer. In addition to the *akbaalía*, the sponsor and a
respected elder also offer prayers during the two subsequent morning sessions. A tremendous amount of emotion
is projected into the words of all three. Tears may come to
the eyes of many as the needs of a loved one and the sacrifices being made are deeply felt.

## Dancing

In dance one's intentions are offered. Dancing, *dissúua*, is
the primary activity for most Sun Dance participants, and
it is considered the most spectacular dimension of the ceremony. Not all questers dance at the same rate, however.
Some, especially women, seldom "charge" the forked tree.
As each participant offers a private vow, so each dances at
his or her own pace, some steadily, most pacing themselves,
a few seldom at all. No stigma is connected with choosing
not to "charge" the Buffalo or the Eagle as frequently as
others do. In fact, younger men are often advised "not to
take it too fast" during their first few dances. Some women
insist that it is not proper for a woman to dance at all, that
"dancing is for the men." Dancing, like prayer, is thus an
individual endeavor.

Each dancer has a "starting gate," a space around the
inner wall of the lodge in which to position himself or herself. On the second full day of the dance, willow and, occasionally, pine saplings twelve to fifteen feet long are brought
into the lodge and planted a few inches in the ground and
two feet apart from each other just in front of the dancers.
Thick green foliage is left on the tops, and the bark is
stripped from the trunks to provide a smooth grip for the
dancers. The saplings are linked in a continuous chain with
bundles of willows, which are tied to the poles at a height
just above the heads of the dancers.

The men are dressed in their brightly colored skirts and
beaded belts, many with Ermine skins or other medicine
objects draped from their necks. The women are wearing
their best calico dresses and engraved leather belts. When

## THE LITTLE FEATHERS

Under the heat of the Sun, it being an unusually hot day, the dancers are suffering and "drying up." One man has been dancing "hard," continuously for some time and has just laid back in his stall for a little rest. He's danced in the Big Lodge numerous times over the years, giving of himself in fulfillment of his vows, but *xapáaliia* has never been bestowed upon him. An *akbaalía*, the man "running" this Sun Dance, is up and dancing. Focusing on a particular part of the forked tree, he "charges" and dances back from it as a host of others do likewise, many with Ermine hung from their necks, all with Eagle plumes in hand. Each maintains a direct path between himself and the center pole, none blocking the path of another. The sounds of the singers beside their drum and of the Eagle-bone whistles tipped with the Bird's plume pierce the air. Charging and dancing, they continue under the Sun's watch.

Suddenly, from the shoulder and near the ear of the *akbaalía*, a voice is heard. "When you finish your Dance tomorrow, before you go out of this Dance, I want you to give your Little Feathers, that you work on people with, I want you to give them to that man lying right over there."

The Father of the *akbaalía*, his Iilápxe, has spoken. After the *akbaalía* sits down in his stall, he motions in Indian sign language to the man, telling him he has been "chosen" to receive this *xapáaliia*. As the dancers leave the lodge, the gift of the Feathers is made. It's his "reward" for all he has given in past Sun Dances. The Iilápxe has deemed him sincere, a man who will use the Feathers for "good purposes." He will now "sit on the shoulders" of his new son.

dancing, all face the center pole, whistles to their lips. Songs are being sung by those gathered around the bass drum, which stands just inside the entrance to the lodge. At times, the male singers are accompanied by a row or two of female singers, who sit in one or two rows immediately behind the men. They tap sprigs of willow branches on the ground to the beat of the song. Seated in front of the singers may be an old man, who urges the dancers to dance "hard" and continuously. At the start of each song, with Eagle plumes in hand, some dancers "charge" the forked tree, while many look on, seated in their stalls. During a "charge," some dancers come closer to the pole than others, thus accommodating the many dancers in such tight quarters. No one is to cross in front of another. As those who have charged dance back to their stalls, still blowing their whistles, they continue to face the tree.

One who is dancing continuously watches a single spot on the center pole. It may be the Buffalo, the Eagle, or the Little Old Man, who is sometimes seen seated in the crotch of the tree. A person who is dancing "hard" may see the object on which he is focusing "finally move and show itself to the person." The Eagle may begin to dance alongside one as he "charges" and dances back from the center pole. The Buffalo may "chase" a dancer, knocking him down. When this happens, the dancer is said to have taken a "hard fall." None disturb a fallen dancer. An *akbaalía* prays over him and places sweet sage or cattail reeds on the still body. As the fallen dancer lies on the ground, he receives a vision; he "sees something." It may be himself, a bird, an animal, or something that he is "looking for." Different people hear and see different images. When the dancer awakes, he may tell a brother, a clan uncle, or an *akbaalía* of the vision, or he may keep the vision private. Inevitably, the dancer will stand up and continue dancing, renewed and fresh. Those who suffer, those who "dry up," those who are *diakaashe* will receive "something." Their vows will be answered in some way.

Participants "charge" and dance back away from the center pole while blowing their Eagle-bone whistles to the beat of the drum and the singers.

## A HARD FALL

It's his fourth Sun Dance, completing the cycle he'd pledged
three years before. He wakes that morning of the second day
feeling "secure, at home," his grandfather and brother on either
side of him. Today he'll dance.

It's not an unusually hot late July morning, perhaps in the
upper eighties, when he and a host of others begin "charging" the
center pole. The song offered by the singers is "strong and steady."
Several are gathered by the lodge door looking on. His focus is to
be the Buffalo that faces him, looking west, and the Buffalo's gaze
is on him. With Eagle plumes in hand, an old whistle given him
by his grandmother in his lips, and with *díakaashe*, he "charges"
the Buffalo and dances back to his stall, "charges" again and dances
back to the beat of the drum. Again and again he "charges." After
some time, unaware of how much, and several songs later, he begins to feel even more "secure, at home." Any concern he may
have had for his mortal being, for his personal safety is completely gone. Harder he dances. Others begin to recognize what's
taking place, as one by one they give up their "charges" for his.
The singers continue with greater fervor, their song accompanying his movements. Those at the door begin taking notice as well.
As his "charges" become more determined, his bodily strength
drains. His once straight path to and from the center pole now
wavers. As he returns each time from his "charge," he falls hard
against his stall of cottonwood saplings. His brother stands and
lends his strength to that of the stall by bracing it. He loses all
sense of time and place, keeping only his thoughts of his vow, and
of the Buffalo.

And then it happens. With the force of the Buffalo, he takes a
"hard fall." His body lies there on the ground as if lifeless. The
song stops. His brother and another run to the middle of the
dance area, to his side, and place cattail reeds over him and sweet
sage at his head. The dance will go on now, but with one less
dancer.

He journeys now with the clear awareness that he's without his
physical body. It lies there in the lodge, becoming ever more removed from him. He finds himself in a deep canyon, as distinctly
"jagged" rocks crown the walls on each side of him. He looks always to the sky, searching for "something" but not knowing what
it is he's seeking. The sky is empty above him. The canyon is deep
and "dark," the rocks very "hard" about him. Then he's in a pine

forest with towering trees, and again he sees a "jagged" horizon to the sky, as he continues his search. But the sky is without form. He then finds himself in a grove of green cottonwoods, textured with a "round" contour as it opens to the sky, but a sky only very clear and blue. And then he's no longer looking up, but is himself up, among the clouds. The white clouds flow through the sky, "soft and rounded." He continues to look for "something" but sees only the blanket of cloud all about him. And then he realizes that what he's seeking will not be seen "out there"; no animal will reveal itself to him, coming to him as such. As he floats with the clouds, looking about, he realizes he has the ears and horns of the Buffalo; he's looking about through the Buffalo's eyes. He and the Buffalo are one. Nothing is to be seen "out there," for it's occurred in him.

He wakes in his own body, the dance going on around him. An *akbaalía* listens, as the young man relates his journey. He's then told of the vision's significance, and cautioned "never to eat of the buffalo." During the feast following the Sun Dance, at which buffalo meat is served, he gives gifts to the sponsor and the *akbaalía* who have helped prepare the way for, and counseled him in, his vision. In return for his gifts, the most important of which is associated with *díakaashe*, he's given the Buffalo medicine.

To dance is to fast, to give up one's own water, to "dry up" (*bilisshíissannee*). In the 115-degree heat of the dance, the dancers give up their own water as it drips from the tips of their whistles. Under the heat of the sun the dancers' throats and tongues may swell, and their stomachs and legs may cramp. During the Sun Dance, dancers offer up their own water in exchange for the "cool and wet" qualities of *baaxpée*.

After a dancer has "taken a hard fall" and received a vision, he becomes "cool and refreshed" and can resume dancing with intensity. An *akbaalía* can draw water from the forked tree with his Eagle feathers. When a dancer is suffering "too much," an *akbaalía* can "touch him up," allowing water to come to a parched throat. Water may be sprayed from the whistle of an *akbaalía* over the back of one who is suffering. One dancer said that the water "felt like an icicle going into my back." When the day is extremely hot and all are suffering, an *akbaalía* may bring cooling clouds from over a hill to refresh the dancers. For some, a particular song may bring water to their Eagle-bone whistles and moisten their dry throats.

On the second full day of the dance, when the dancers are likely to begin to suffer, aid is rendered. The friends and relatives who have camped nearby reciprocate for what the dancers are sacrificing on their behalf. In the morning, the willow-pole stalls are constructed for each dancer. White sheets can be wrapped around the slender poles of the stalls to offer shade during the hottest part of the day. The stall can brace a weakened dancer between "charges." Bundles of cattail reeds, sweet "man sage," and mint are brought in. Tired dancers lie on and under the greenery and are refreshed. The smell of the "man sage" and the mint is refreshing to those whose senses have been heightened by the fast.

## Doctoring

In doctoring, or *baalía*, which occurs on the second full day of the ceremony, one's intentions are answered. On this day

## A COOL WIND

It's only Saturday morning, two days to go, but everyone senses this Dance will be a "rough one." By ten, their worst fears are coming true; the temperature is already approaching ninety degrees and climbing fast. One of the dancers, an old woman, calls to her great-granddaughter standing just on the other side of the brush wall. "Go tell the 'old man' to make some wind to cool things down a bit." The girl quickly runs to a small wall-tent west of the lodge and relates what's needed. Inside, the "old man" "makes medicine." Soon, a gentle breeze begins blowing in from the northwest. The cooler air brings hope for a pleasant day. The breeze continues into the early afternoon. But as it does, it also begins to pick up speed. Soon the overhead rafters are swaying back and forth. Then, on the west side of the lodge, some of the heavy pine brush falls on a couple of the dancers. "Go tell the 'old man' to stop the wind." In the small tent, prayers are again given. And as they are, the wind dies down.

many "cooling" *baaxpée* gifts are distributed. Individuals not participating in the dancing line up at the entrance to the Big Lodge and tell the "announcer" of their needs. The "announcer" calls an *akbaalía*, who brings his Eagle-feather fan to the center pole. In addition to the *akbaalía* running the dance, there will be other *akbaalía* among those dancing. They also may be asked to doctor. Either singly or in small groups, and all barefoot, those in need gather at the center pole, facing east. The *akbaalía* stands immediately behind them and "touches them up" individually with his Eagle-feather fan after asking each to name his or her affliction. As prayer is given to the Iilápxe, *baaxpée* "pulsates" from the center pole to the fan, then on to the ailment of the person in need. Each feels a "cooling sensation" as the *baaxpée* penetrates his or her body. As the fan is jerked away from the person's body, the affliction is taken away and "tossed to the east, gone with the wind."

## The Return

Preparations begin early in the morning of the third day for the departure from the Big Lodge. Midday is the usual time for completing the dance. Water from a "pure spring" is collected in large water coolers or in new trash cans. The need for such a quantity of water is great. After it is brought in by a group of women designated by the sponsor, the water is blessed at the center pole and distributed to each participant. Each dancer, parched from three days of "drying up," receives several cups of the life-giving water and is refreshed. Then prayers are given. Clan uncles and aunts and *akbaalía* stand behind groups of dancers in the lodge and offer prayer for each who has "blown the whistle." The dancers give blankets and quilts to those who helped them complete the fast. As they leave the lodge, the dancers may be given cool watermelon and soda pop by the sponsor's family.

During the afternoon or on the following day, the sponsor gives a feast for all the dancers, their families, and any others present. Among the various foods served will inevitably be buffalo steak, fry bread, and watermelon. This feast is the sponsor's final obligation for the Sun Dance, his final gift to Akbaatatdía.

## Sun Dance and World View

The "driftwood" world view is revealed through the Apsáalooke Sun Dance. As the driftwood bundle is tightly interwoven, so are the Sun Dancers. Each dancer is linked to family for encouragement and refreshment and to the lodge with its center pole, Eagle, Buffalo, and Little Old Man. The linkage becomes animated when the dancer "drys up" and offers his or her sincerity. In exchange for what is offered, a prayer can be channeled, a vision received, or a cure obtained. A daughter is given health, or a young man is guided by the Buffalo during a vision. The meaning and life-force of the transcendent are brought to bear upon and realized within the participants of the Sun Dance.

# CHAPTER 7

# Application of *Xapáaliia*

BECAUSE THE SUN DANCE religion focuses on offering a means to, rather than a prescription of, the spiritual, *xapáaliia* is a private expression of one's relationship with the transcendent. No one else can share a person's vision or be adopted by his or her Iilápxe. Others, however, can be affected by one's *xapáaliia*, as many are when they are doctored by an *akbaalía*. The emphasis of the Sun Dance religion is on providing the means to a goal, the goal being the application of *baaxpée* to the human domain. Not only does the Sun Dance religion allow access to the power and wisdom emanating from Akbaatatdía, but once the power has been realized within an individual, it facilitates its dispersal into the lives of all other Apsáalooke.

Medicine affects people's lives. Its form may be an answer to the prayers one has given during a sweat bath, or it may be the gift of *xapáaliia* itself, given for what was sacrificed during a fast. It may involve being "shot" by someone using "bad medicine." It may involve the use of "love medicine" to bring about the sexual conquest of a desired woman. It may mean consistently winning the hand-game tournaments for one's district. Most frequently it is a gift of health obtained during a bundle opening or while prayer is being said. Medicine alters people's lives in both subtle and dramatic ways, sometimes detrimentally but more often beneficially. Medicine transforms.

In the buffalo days, medicine was used for a variety of purposes. William Wildschut, in *Crow Indian Medicine*

## THE TWO BULLETS

A fight breaks out in one of the Indian bars off the reservation. A gun is pulled, and a young man lies shot in a pool of blood. Without hesitation, his friends take him to the Indian Health Service hospital. But because the man has lost a lot of blood and because the two bullets are lodged dangerously near his heart, the doctors are reluctant to operate. A specialist will be brought in. The parents of the boy, knowing that help is available now, seek out an *akbaalía*. That evening the *akbaalía* goes to the man's hospital room. As it's a late hour, few will be around to disturb them. Standing at the man's bedside, the old man pulls back the bandages very carefully so as not to cause any discomfort. The powder of a particular root is all he has with him. It's part of his *xapáaliia*, given to him by his Iilápxe. He gently pours some of the powder into each of the wounds and places the bandages back in their proper position. Praying, the *akbaalía* stays with the young man through the night and into the early morning. It's all he can do. The next morning the nurses come into the room to change the dressings, but what they find as they pull back the sheets are the two bullets lying beside the man; "they'd come out the same way they'd gone in." X-rays are taken, finding no sign of the bullets, and as soon as the boy regains his strength he's allowed to go home.

*Bundles,* lists ten categories of medicine bundles used in former times: Sun Dance, War, Shield, Skull, Rock, Medicine Pipe, Love, Witchcraft, Healing, and Hunting (1975: 16–17). Although many of these bundles overlapped in function, the application of medicine during the buffalo days was much more varied than it is today.

Medicine is still applied to a variety of endeavors, such as controlling the weather, a woman, or the outcome of a hand game, but its applications today fall into three broad categories: (1) preventive, (2) doctoring, and (3) gambling. Reliance on medicine has not necessarily diminished since the buffalo days. Medicine is still as pervasively integrated into the lives of traditional families as it was into the lives of their ancestors. Wildschut's classification of medicine was derived from an analysis of the contents as well as the application of the medicine bundles. While many of the bundles discussed by Wildschut are still employed today— Sun Dance, Rock, Medicine Pipe, Witchcraft, and Healing—the discussion here focuses on the functional application of medicine bundles.

Any medicine has the *potential* to be used for prevention, gambling, or doctoring. When a bundle is opened, the purpose for which the *baaxpée* is applied often depends on the intent of the opener. In *practice,* however, most *xapáaliia* forms are used for prevention, while fewer are applied for doctoring or gambling.

## Preventive Use

After the *suuwassée* (first thunder) in the spring, or on each evening of the full moon, medicine bundles may be opened. The contents are smudged with sweet cedar, and prayers for the general welfare of the family are given. The prayer, which is said aloud, offers thanks for past blessings and asks that they continue. The Iilápxe are asked to watch over all the relatives to see that all remain in good health and that none become victims of "bad medicine."

The primary role of many medicine bundles is preventive—to care for the general well-being and to prevent mis-

The Indian Health Service Hospital at Crow Agency.

fortune. Although many people have medicine, few of them consider it appropriate, or their medicine powerful enough, to doctor the sick. For example, one man who has Squirrel medicine would rather seek the aid of an *akbaalía* than use his own medicine to treat an affliction. His *xapáaliia* is to be used to provide food, not to cure. Some families may possess medicine that was initially acquired by a distant ancestor. With the passage of time the specific instructions for, and meanings of, the medicine may have become blurred. Only a general sense of *baaxpée* remains. In such cases it is unwise to apply the medicine for a specific reason, as in doctoring. A taboo may be broken, or a restriction overlooked, causing injury instead of benefit. But the bundle is, nevertheless, opened periodically and smudged while a prayer for prevention is offered.

One form of preventive application of *xapáaliia* has not become blurred over the years, however. As medicine during the buffalo days was taken into battle against the Cheyenne or the Lakota on a war shield or hung around a warrior's neck, so it has been taken into battle against the Germans, the Japanese, the North Koreans, and the Vietcong.

## One Who Doctors (Akbaalía)

The most important application of *xapáaliia* is in doctoring, or what is termed *baalía* (to doctor) and *hawassée* (to cure). For many Sun Dance–oriented Apsáalooke, the *akbaalía* (one who doctors) is the primary agent of the doctoring application. The noun *baaxpáak*, meaning "one who has *baaxpée*," is also used to refer to such a person. While many are credited with a *xapáaliia* that can affect a particular affliction, only a few are recognized as *akbaalía*.

In attempting to describe what an *akbaalía* is and does, the combined Euro-American categories of doctor, priest, counselor, and friend only begin to approximate the function. An *akbaalía* is, first of all, a human being. He or she laughs and cries and loves and hates just as others do. He or she is a responsible parent and is generous and caring toward both child and elder. Nothing is psychologically or socially unusual about an *akbaalía*. Any Apsáalooke man or woman has the potential to become an *akbaalía*.

To designate someone an *akbaalía* is in many ways vague and misleading. Simply possessing *medicine* is not synonymous with being a *medicine* man. Many who are not *akbaalía* regularly use a medicine bundle. For some, "medicine" means knowledge of the medicinal properties of a particular leaf, which, when made into a tea and taken regularly, may prevent a cold or cure bleeding ulcers. The power to stop a hemorrhage has been given to certain young men. Certain women have the skill to treat colicky babies or to rid a child of an earache. In all of these cases, however, *xapáaliia* is applied for a specialized purpose and only for that purpose. The tea, for instance, cannot treat arthritis or a backache. Although some people have a *xapáaliia* that

## THE WAR SHIELD

Just before leaving for Vietnam, he stops in for a visit with his "adopted grandparents." As he departs, memories of a wonderful evening go with him, along with a small pouch hung from his neck.

On two separate occasions, his platoon is ambushed by the Vietcong. Many of those he commands, many of his friends, are killed. His frustration and anger are noticed by his superiors, who keep him "out of the action for a while." He asks if he can go out, not far from camp, and offer a prayer in "the Indian way." His request is granted.

It's a warm, humid day and the cool spring water that runs beside the trail is inviting. Setting his helmet and rifle against a tree, he stoops over and cups some refreshment in his hands. As he does, and not more than a few feet away, a Vietcong jumps from a tree, rifle in hand. The man immediately lunges for his own weapon, but as he stands, the bullet hits him squarely in the chest. The impact knocks him back into the water. He waits. He remembers what had been told in basic training: "you won't feel anything at first, and then it'll hit." He waits, but only the water running over him is felt. He looks down at his chest and sees his khakis and t-shirt torn away. But that's as far as the bullet has penetrated. "There's no blood, not even a scratch." He stands, and as he does, an amazed attacker throws his rifle to the ground and runs off.

Upon returning to the reservation, he shows the shirt to the "grandparents," and gives thanks for a small pouch.

The Bighorn Mountains, five miles west of Wyola.

can treat a particular problem more effectively than anyone else, they cannot be considered *akbaalía* simply because they have *xapáaliia*.

In conceptualizing *akbaalía*, one must think in terms of degree. Among all Apsáalooke who have medicine, whether acknowledged as *akbaalía* or not, no qualitative differences exist in their activities or their relationships with the transcendent. The manner in which *xapáaliia* is received, whether during a fast, during a Sun Dance, or through inheritance, may be very similar among all who possess it. The ritual application of *xapáaliia* as in a bundle opening or in the Sun Dance, may also be similar from individual to individual. Every bundle is endowed with *baaxpée*. The distinction is in the *amount* of medicine and accompanying ritual activity.

An *akbaalía* will likely have several Iilápxe and thus a variety of medicine aids at his or her disposal. A particular Iilápxe, however, may be of special importance and, possibly, reside within the body of the *akbaalía*. The *xapáaliia* of an *akbaalía* can affect a wide assortment of afflictions. An *akbaalía* may be called on to doctor a broken arm that is slow to set, a sore that is slow to heal, a cold that persists, or a cancer that continues to grow. His or her advice will be sought on what to do about a son who drinks too much, an employer who is demanding, or a course of action that needs to be decided on. An *akbaalía* would not use *xapáaliia* to injure another person. As one *akbaalía* explained: "My idea is to try and help. I'd never think about trying to do anything out of the way to hurt somebody." An *akbaalía* should used medicine only for "good" purposes. On the second day of the Sun Dance, an *akbaalía* may be asked to doctor at the center pole. In most circumstances, an *akbaalía* has the "authority" to "run" a prayer meeting, the ceremonial doctoring session. The authority to do this is generally recognized by the larger community and derived originally from another *akbaalía* and one's own Iilápxe. In the final analysis, if one is to be called *akbaalía,* it is because people have put their trust in that person and are confident about the strength and effectiveness of his or her *xapáaliia*.

Like the Sun Dance religion itself, the *akbaalía* functions more as a facilitator than as a prescriber. He or she assists individuals in gaining access to *baaxpée* so that they can acquire a vision or be doctored. The *akbaalía* does not really prescribe a doctrinal position on the nature of the spiritual. While the *akbaalía* help interpret dreams and visions, the visions have already been given. The doctrinal position of the vision stems from its spiritual source and simply needs to be clarified by the *akbaalía*. The *akbaalía* act as guides to the transcendent.

### Opening of the Medicine Bundles (*Xapáalialustuua*)

Doctoring is often associated with *xapáalialustuua* (opening of the medicine bundles), or what is sometimes called a "prayer meeting." These are held as often as twice a month, often during a full moon, and are considered by many to be an extension of the Sun Dance. Those who sit in the "prayer circle" have danced numerous times in the Big Lodge. While a sponsor organizes a prayer meeting, prompted by his own illness or the illness of a family member, all are welcome to attend and can be doctored at the meeting. The number attending the ceremony may range from a handful to as many as sixty. People have been known to travel as far as 750 miles to attend a prayer meeting, which may last until the early-morning hours, and then leave immediately after the ceremony to begin their trip back home.

### Sun Dance Doctoring

Doctoring is an integral part of the Sun Dance. The health and well-being of family members are utmost in the thoughts of the dancers, and this concern is expressed as the *akbaalía* directs his Eagle-feather fan. Standing before the center pole, through which prayers have been given and visions received, an *akbaalía* fans the bodies of children and grandparents, attempting to remove whatever afflicts them. Both child and grandparent are touched by *baaxpée*.

### Extended Doctoring

For one who is in need of immediate assistance but cannot attend a bundle opening or a Sun Dance, other means of doctoring exist. Almost always the *akbaalía* will come to the patient if the patient is unable to come to the *akbaalía*. Indian Health Service (IHS) physicians would be amazed if they knew the extent of Indian doctoring that occurs inside hospitals. *Akbaalía* are some of the most regular visitors of the IHS patients.

One *akbaalía* has *xapáaliia* to doctor "long distance," be the patient in New York, California, or even Europe. He builds a small fire and sprinkles sweet cedar over the hot coals. Taking his Eagle feathers, he calls on his *Iilápxe*. A "smoke" is offered, during which he tells of his patient's needs. He asks the Fathers to go to the patient and "represent" him, doing the work he would normally do in person.

## A PRAYER MEETING

In the large living room, the *akbaalía*, along with four of his helpers, three men and a woman, his "right-hand men," sit cross-
legged on the floor. A partial circle is thus formed opening to the
east, from where life emerges each morning and toward which
the wind blows. In front of those who sit in the "prayer circle" lie
opened medicine bundles. Each individual has carefully unwrap-
ped or brought out the tangible images of his personal *xapáaliia*,
including a leather effigy of an Elk anchored in a tray of brown
earth; the skins of an Otter, an Elk, and an Ermine; a small,
round mirror; and several Eagle-feather fans. Hot coals from a
fire are brought in on a frying pan and with the sprinkling of
sweet cedar, the room is filled with a pleasant smell. The room
itself, those in the "prayer circle," the objects that lie upon the
floor, and those seeking help all become engulfed and blessed
with the spiritual. Eagle-feather fans are "renewed" with *baaxpée* as they are incensed. An avenue to the Maker is thus opened.

Standing, with eyes closed and arms outstretched to the east,
the *akbaalía* offers the opening prayer. As the words are spoken
by the *akbaalía*, his "medicine song" is sung by several singers
who sit to his right, gathered around their bass drum. After the
prayer, several people come forward to give "smokes" and requests. After receiving them all, each person in the "prayer
circle" smokes a cigarette, giving its prayer. "As the smoke ascends, so will prayer ascend" to Akbaatatdía. With a confidence,
the drum beat and Sun Dance songs accompany the prayers.
Then another "smoke" is lit from the fire of the previous and a
continuous chain of prayer ascends. By midnight all of the requests have been sent and a short "intermission" follows.

With the penetrating beat of the drum, the Sun Dance singers
resume their songs. The *akbaalía* stands at the opening of the
"prayer circle," facing east. Those who have come to be "worked
on" come forward in turn. They include one with a paralysis from
a stroke, one with a kidney infection, another with only a cold.
All face the life-giving east. For each person the *akbaalía* offers a
prayer, asking the assistance of his Iilápxe. It's their images, the
*xapáaliia*, that've been laid on the floor for all to see. As his fan of
Eagle feathers "touches up" each patient from "head to foot," the
power "pulsates" into the fan, then into the right hand, arm, and
from there into the entire body of the *akbaalía*. Then as the
feathers "touch" each patient, they too feel the "pulsation." The

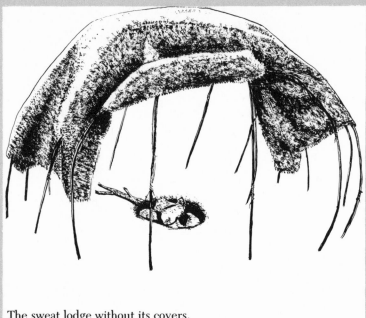

The sweat lodge without its covers.

*akbaalía* directs the Feathers with great care, gently fanning and patting the body. Each person feels a "cooling" sensation, the strength of the Feathers and the warmth of the hand of the *akbaalía*. More sweet cedar is added to the coals and the singing continues uninterrupted, uniting all in a common bond. After several minutes, the "pulsation" begins to slow, and the fan is jerked away from the person's body. The "trouble is tossed to the east, letting it blow away from the person's body, away from this house, gone with the wind." Those who give of themselves, trusting in the *baaxpée* of the Iilápxe and in Akbaatatdía will be rewarded.

After doctoring all who had come this evening, the *akbaalía* asks one among the onlookers if he would like to be "worked on." As the young man stands facing east, a prayer is said aloud and the *akbaalía* "touches him up" with his Little Feathers. The "cooling warmth" penetrates his head at the touch. His entire body is fanned, but the *baaxpée* concentrates itself in the young man's head.

During a sweat bath several days earlier the same young man had asked for guidance. Two men entered the small, dome-shaped lodge, clothed only in the darkness of the evening. Once they were inside, the door was lowered, sealing off the sights, sounds, and movements of the world they had been a part of a few moments before. The water was then poured over the heated rocks which glowed red from the "fire" within them, and prayers were given as the steam rose. In a pit just to the left of the door were the rocks, which had been "cooked" over cottonwood logs that afternoon. Just before the sweat, they were placed with great care inside the lodge. The hot vapors penetrated the young man's body, cleansing him "from the inside out," and he "switched" himself, his back, shoulders, and arms with a short bundle of willow cuttings. As the intensity of the heat grew, he gave of himself, of his bodily comfort, so that his prayers might be better heard. As the young man prayed aloud, of the many things he asked one was direction and understanding as to his course in life. A particular problem needed solving. In the Small Lodge, the "brother" of the Big Lodge, an *akbaalía* shared in a prayer and the young man's life.

Now, during the bundle opening, this same *akbaalía* helps the young man find direction through the power and wisdom of his Iilápxe.*

---

*The bundle opening described took place in April, 1975, and illustrates the ritual process of applying medicine. For additional commentary on the prayer meeting see Voget (1984) and Fitzgerald (forthcoming).

## THE TREE'S WATER

It's the second full day, an extremely hot day, and all but a few of the fasters seek any cooling shade offered by the Big Lodge.

Most of the participants, over a hundred in all, drape light-colored sheets from their stalls to cool themselves a little. Despite the heat, some are naked before the Sun, either "charging" the center pole or being "touched up" by the Eagle feathers of an *akbaalía*.

At the door of the lodge stand many people, Indians and non-Indians, of various ages and needs. Some bring small children to be blessed and prayed for. Others seek a cure for arthritis, gall-stones, or diabetes. In addition to those at the door, many of the dancers also come forth. Either singly or in small groups, those in need will have an *akbaalía* called to the center pole by the "announcer." Exhausted by the fast and by the loss of strength "given out" to those "worked on," an *akbaalía* makes his way to the center pole. Those seeking help enter the lodge barefoot and stand facing the forked tree and the east, with the *akbaalía* immediately behind them. With his Eagle-feather fan in his right hand, the *akbaalía* "touches up" each person from "head to foot." Prayer is always given and the "pulsating" power is felt as it moves from the center pole to the fan and the *akbaalía* and then into the body of the person being "worked on." Song offered by the singers continues uninterrupted as a person stands before the forked tree. On this day many tears are shed by those "touched up" and by those who feel the suffering of the fasters.

This Sun Dance is a "rough one," and the 115 degree afternoon heat of the Sun "dries up" everyone, and many are suffering. As one dancer says, "All I can spit is cotton." Just after the Sunrise ceremony, the slender poles of cottonwood had been planted around the inner perimeter of the lodge. With the tips left covered with green leaves and tied together with bundles of willows, the poles form a continuous chain of stalls that can brace each dancer between his "charges." By mid-afternoon many lie in the meager shade offered by the north side of the lodge, while their cramped legs or stomach muscles are being massaged by relatives. An *akbaalía* inserts long sweet-sage stems into the throat of a dancer who is suffering from dry heaves. Throughout the day, families and friends of those inside bring sweet "man-sage," mint cuttings, and cattail reeds, all tied in small bundles, to the fasters. By their pleasant smell and cooling touch, the gifts

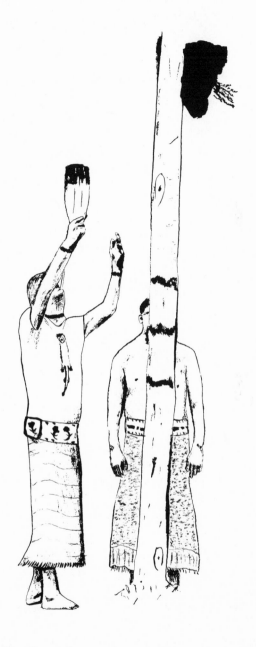

An *akbaalia* "touches up" a patient with his fan of Eagle feathers as the Buffalo looks on.

help refresh the participants. Some fasteners call out to the singers, asking that their medicine song be sung. As the song is sung, water may come to their Eagle-bone whistles, and they receive some relief. But still many suffer.

That evening, as several "charge" the center pole, an old man stands alone before the forked tree. With a small fan of Eagle feathers, he prays to Akbaatatdía and the Tree for aid. In the cooler evening air, more fasters are up and dancing "hard." The song continues as a large number of onlookers watch from the door. At one of the tree's knots, just to the left of and below the Buffalo, a few drops of water emerge. The *akbaalía* continues the prayer. More water emerges. A cup is filled with the life of the Tree and given to the sponsor of the dance to drink. He's an elderly man paralyzed by a stroke. Others crowd around the center pole and receive at least a drop or two of the Tree's water. The next day, as the Buffalo is being removed from his watch, a few drops of water can still be seen in the knot. The aid sought by the old man, an *akbaalía*, has been given.*

*In July, 1975, this doctoring segment of the Ashkísshe was observed.

Because they can "travel by lightning," the Iilápxe are able to "touch up" a sick person immediately, no matter where that person is.

### Efficacy

The efficacy of medicine is directly related to the recipient's "belief" (*ammaakalátche*) in it. If a "cure" (*baalía*) is to be effective, the patient must "believe" in it. To appreciate the Apsáalooke act of "believing" and, as a consequence, the effectiveness of an *akbaalía* and his or her associated *xapáaliia*, the Apsáalooke world view must be considered.

The efficacy of *baaxpée* presupposes a contextual relationship between tangible and transcendent occurrences. The rituals observed and the objects revealed when a medicine bundle is opened replicate a correspondence occurring on the transcendent plane. As a bundle is opened, exposing Eagle feathers and a leather Elk effigy, as a fan of feathers is brushed gently over someone's shoulders and back, as a bitter-tasting "brew" is drunk, as words of prayer are offered, the objects and actions symbolically mirror what is transpiring on the spiritual plane. The Eagle-feather fan is a means to, and a manifestation of, the Eagle's meaning and strength, its *baaxpée*. It is an outlet through which the spiritual spills forth into the manifest. But the flow is carefully directed by the hand and intention of the *akbaalía*. The movement of the fan makes a design for the application of *baaxpée*. During a bundle opening, the *akbaalía* thus visually and dramatically expresses and links both the physical and the spiritual levels of reality. An *akbaalía* guides his Eagle feathers, channeling the transcendent into the material and attempting to effect a cure. At the same time his *xapáaliia* identifies and attests to the volition and omnipotence of the transcendent as the Eagle feathers are displayed in hand.

The efficacy of *baaxpée* also presupposes a dynamics in this contextual relationship. As discussed earlier, the idea of reciprocity dominates many human, and almost all spiritual, relationships in Apsáalooke culture.

In the realm of social activities, the institution of give-aways (*ammaakée*) exemplifies this reciprocity. On occasions such as a son's or daughter's graduation, a soldier's return from military duty, the birth or naming of a child, or the celebration of a birthday or of being elected to a public office or winning a basketball championship, a family will publicly show its gratitude to others, especially the *áassahke*. Not a single relative or friend of the honored person goes unrecognized. Each family gives to another and, in turn, is given to; each individual gives to his or her *áassahke* and, in return, receives gifts.

Reciprocity is fundamental to the fast and the Sun Dance. In return for three days of fasting, a gift of *xapáaliia* may be received. Once received, access to the *baaxpée* continues only for as long as the *xapáaliia* is properly cared for. The Iilápxe and the adopted child each look after the other.

In the context of the doctoring ritual, an exchange must also take place for *xapáaliia* to be effective. To receive the benefits of *baaxpée*, one must give something in exchange. After, and sometimes before, a doctoring ceremony, a patient gives money, a blanket, or something of monetary value to the *akbaalía*. Some *akbaalía* require that such gifts be given in quantities of four (four blankets or four five-dollar bills, for example). But these exchanges involve only human beings. The Iilápxe also must receive a gift. While a blanket helps establish the necessary relationship with the *akbaalía*, it is not sufficient to do so with the Iilápxe.

The most valuable gift one can give the Iilápxe is that associated with *díakaashe*. This word describes an inner disposition characterized by pride and sincerity, a state of being that allows a participant to persevere and to perform a difficult sacrifice with determination and vigor. During a fast, "doing it with sincerity," *díakaashe*, is the ultimate basis on which the Iilápxe judge who will receive *xapáaliia*. The act of *díakaashe* possesses a spiritual quality no worldly possession can share.

During a medicine-bundle opening, Iilápxe are present,

The Crow Tribal Government Building, near Crow Agency.

and a channel to *baaxpée* is open as the *akbaalía* directs the Eagle feathers with great care. The patient, in turn, makes a public commitment (*ammaakalátche*) and offers both tangible gifts—blankets—and a spiritual gift—*díakaashe*. In exchange for these gifts the affliction is "tossed to the east, gone with the wind." As when a person receives a vision, one realizes the transcendent within oneself by offering the gift of an inner disposition.

### Gambling and Other Applications

Besides being used for the health and well-being of others, *baaxpée* is applied to other domains of human activity as well. Medicine can be directed toward affecting the "natural course" of events, such as the weather or the attentions

## HAND-GAME MEDICINE

The Kiowa hand-game team is up from Oklahoma, challenging the six district teams on the reservation. They're undefeated, and about to play the weakest of all the Apsáalooke teams. In the school gym the stage is set. The Apsáalooke sit in their bleachers and anticipate the worst—that is, all but one. On the floor the two teams face one another. Among the Kiowa, one stands and begins to sing his medicine song, "making medicine for his team." He's the key to their success. Just as he's about to finish, a man on the top row of the bleachers reaches out with his hand and grabs at the air in the direction of the Kiowa team. The singer immediately stops his song and looks around in wonder. All he can do now is sit down; his power is gone. The Apsáalooke team, "the poorest on the reservation," beats those Kiowas.

## *XAPÁALIIA* THAT SEES

He's just about given up all hope of finding his daughter. The various state agencies have all but stopped their active search for the girl, who has been missing for several weeks now. Perhaps it's in desperation, but the non-Indian rancher goes to an Indian friend and asks if he knows of anyone who can help him. He does. The rancher is told to bring four gifts. Upon doing so, he's introduced to a middle-aged woman. She agrees to do what she can. The Apsáalooke woman goes back with the rancher to his place and that evening sleeps in the car of the girl. She receives a dream and the following morning tells where the girl's body can be found. It's in a gully not far from the ranch.

of the opposite sex. In the latter instance, a woman at a public gathering may be leery of accepting a cup of coffee from a young man whose intentions are not fully known. She may fear that it contains "love medicine." Prayer is often directed toward asking for good weather for an extended journey. If an unexpected and heavy spring snow falls, making a journey difficult, prayer for a chinook is offered. Within a few hours the prayers may be answered. During a Sun Dance, prayer is given to keep the rains away yet to have a few clouds overhead and a light breeze to "cool things off just a bit." One *akbaalía* is known for her *xapáaliia,* which finds lost articles or even missing people. This *akbaalía* is also recognized for her ability to "see," to know what is going on in some distant place. When a ruling is being handed down by a judge in Sheridan, the moment those in the courtroom hear it, she, over one hundred miles away, also knows it.

Although not as frequent an application of *baaxpée* as healing, competitive and gambling-related applications run a close second. While horse races and hand-game tournaments typify such applications, *xapáaliia* has also been used in the heat of a high school basketball competition.

Dating from the buffalo days and still very popular, hand games involve hiding and guessing the locations of objects. They are games of skill and deception, the object being to trick the opposing team's guesser. The guesser on each team often has *xapáaliia* that is clearly designated for hand games. In fact, to have the "right to guess" in a hand game one should have such medicine.

### Xapáaliia and World View

The "driftwood" world view is expressed in the application of *xapáaliia.* With the bundle opened and the objects exposed, the *xapáaliia* is an aperture to the transcendent. As the *akbaalía* "touches up" a person with the Eagle-feather fan, the individual becomes linked to the *baaxpée* for a cure, for a decision, for a life. In exchange for sincerity, for

## BASKETBALL *XAPÁALIIA*

The score is tied with three seconds left in the game. The twenty-foot jump shot rolls around the rim, and rolls once more as everyone watches breathlessly. From among the crowd, someone points his finger at the ball. It rolls in, and the team wins the championship game.

## THE RIGHT TO GUESS

Another season of hand-game tournaments has begun, pitting each of the six reservation-district teams against each other. Frank expects to look on with curiosity and perhaps do a little singing for his district, as he's done over the years. He's never actually participated in the guessing or hiding of the bone objects. This year his district starts off "pretty poorly," with the other districts beating his easily. So Frank, thinking he and his district, for that matter, have nothing to lose, tries "his hand at guessing." Sure enough, he has "good luck," and his team begins to win. Soon, Frank becomes the head guesser for his district. But in so doing, Frank also fails to mention one important consideration to his teammates: he doesn't have the "right to guess." Hand-game medicine has never been given to Frank. But he guesses anyway.

Frank's team continues to win, and they advance to the championship. "The pressure is on"; many people put their money on Frank to win for them. Four different people come to him and add their *xapáaliia* to his, or what they think is his. Someone gives him a black handkerchief to tie around his right arm, for instance. Everyone, including his family and friends, is present for the contest. The atmosphere is excited, and all are hopeful.

As the guesser for his district, Frank loses every game. His team ended as it started out.

Frank was never quite sure why he lost. It may have been that he never had the right to guess in the first place. He also adds, "I had too many medicines given to me; they worked against each other." Frank is sure of one thing, though. No one would speak to him for the longest time. Frank never again tries his hand at guessing.

"doing it with determination," the individual feels the "pulsation" penetrate his or her body and remove the affliction. The transcendent, the ultimate life-force and perennial meaning inherent in the Iilápxe and in Akbaatatdía, is brought to bear on the manifest; the human being is connected to the spiritual.

# CHAPTER 8

# The Wagon Wheel

AS EXPLAINED TO ME by Tom Yellowtail, a Sun Dance elder, the world and its peoples are but a huge wagon wheel, an eternal circle traversed by several spokes. The spokes represent the various peoples and religions of the world, each unique unto itself, yet none more important than another. None can be lengthened, none can be shortened, and none can be removed, because each spoke is necessary for the wheel to turn. Each people and each religion are necessary for the whole.

Yet all spokes are united at the wheel's hub by the pervasive Maker, who is shared and touched by all. Though perhaps conceived of differently by each spoke, the Maker nevertheless remains fundamental to the wheel's support and movement.

Although obviously of Euro-American design, the "wagon wheel" is used by the *akbaalía* to communicate a desired image to non-Indians. The wagon wheel also has a tremendous symbolic significance as an image similar to that represented by the medicine-wheel rock configurations found in the Bighorn Mountains and on the northern plains. It is also symbolic of the circle itself. The image of the circle is manifested in many aspects of Plains Indian culture: the camp circle, the tipi, the sweat lodge, the dancers' movement at a powwow, the directional movement of the pipe during prayer. As a Lakota elder, Tyon, explained:

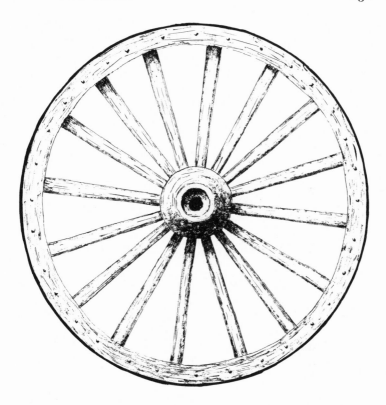

The Wagon Wheel.

The Oglala believe the circle to be sacred because the Great Spirit caused everything in nature to be round except stone. Stone is the implement of destruction. The sun and the sky, the earth and the moon are round like a shield, though the sky is deep like a bowl. Everything that breathes is round like the body of a man. Everything that grows from the ground is round like the stem of a tree. Since the Great Spirit has caused everything to be round mankind should look upon the circle as sacred for it is the symbol of all things in nature except stone. It is also the symbol of the circle that marks the edge of the world and therefore of the four winds that travel there. Consequently, it is also the symbol of a year. The day, the night, and the moon go in a circle above the sky. Therefore the circle is a symbol of these divisions of time and hence the symbol of all time. [Walker 1917:160]

The wagon-wheel imagery thus has an affinity to the immense and primal expression of meaning that is the circle. Because knowledge of the circle's meaning emanates from the perennial meaning inherent in the transcendent, the wagon-wheel image is necessarily *baaxpée*. The image is part of an elder's medicine, part of Yellowtail's vision, and a design by which to live one's life.

## Ashkísshe

Because Tom Yellowtail is a Sun Dance *akbaalía*, it is not surprising that he is so familiar with the wagon-wheel image. After all, in the structure of the Big Lodge and in the movement of the dancers within it, the image of the wagon wheel is clearly visible.

Overhead in the lodge rest the twelve rafters, the spokes, which are anchored to the forked tree, the hub. The center pole is a channel to the Maker. Through it a vision can be received. The Buffalo, hung from the west side of the center pole, may "charge" one, causing a "hard fall," a vision. The Eagle, suspended from the "chief pole" and facing east, may dance alongside a dancer as a guide during a vision journey. The *baaxpée* to doctor and strengthen dancers passes through the center pole. The center pole is the avenue through which dancers direct their prayers to Akbaatatdía and through which their prayers are answered.

As an avenue to the Maker, the forked tree is appropriately adorned with objects that express the omnipresence and life-sustaining power of Akbaatatdía. On it are the flags of day and night, earth and sky; the Eagle, which soars above all and sees all; the Buffalo, whose essence sustains the life of human beings; and the Willows, which offer cool, liquid refreshment. The forked tree is itself a symbol of life, with green foliage at the tip of each fork, towering above all. When the heat of the day becomes intense and the dancers are suffering, an *akbaalía* may draw life-giving water from the Buffalo or from a knot in the Tree with his Feathers. The center pole is like Akbaatatdía, supportive and essential.

Below the twelve rafters and the forked tree the dancers "charge" and dance away from the center pole in fulfillment of their personal vows. Because each vow is unique and individual, each quester dances at his or her own pace, each with his or her own disposition. On the second day of the dance, a day of doctoring during which many gifts are given, each dancer is painted according to his or her own medicine or the medicine of another. The painted designs and the number of "charges" offered by each dancer are distinct and individualized, like the separate spokes on a wagon wheel. The willow-pole stalls discussed earlier are constructed on the morning that the paint is applied. Each stall, and thus each dancer, is no further from, and no closer to, the center pole than any other. All are part of the wheel's rim. No participant crosses the path of another during the dance, for all spokes must radiate from, and lie on a straight course toward, the center pole.

Just as each dancer represents a spoke, each can also represent the hub. When a dancer takes a "hard fall" and the Eagle or the Buffalo dances alongside, the dancer journeys with, and becomes a part of, what he seeks. The dancer's identity merges with the Iilápxe, with Akbaatatdía. As the center pole and the items attached to it are an avenue through which *baaxpée* is channeled, so too is the *akbaalía*. Standing at the forked tree with Eagle-feather fan in hand, the *akbaalía* is an aperture to Akbaatatdía. While a dancer is being "touched up" with the Eagle-feather fan, *baaxpée* extends into his or her body and removes an affliction. *Baaxpée* stirs within the dancer. "As the smoke ascends," not only do the specific intentions of a dancer ascend, but if the dancer is *díakaashe*, his or her sincerity also ascends to Akbaatatdía. In dance, in doctoring, and in prayer each quester's distinctness can be dissolved into a union with the hub, with Akbaatatdía.

The Sun Dance Lodge and the actions of the dancers within it thus symbolically replicate a concept of the world. The Apsáalooke term for Sun Dance, Ashkisshe, although it has additional explanations (Lowie 1983:297), may refer to this symbolism. Ashkísshe literally means "imitation lodge." The structure of the lodge and the ceremonial behavior of the dancers imitate, or mirror, the cosmos perceived by the Apsáalooke. Hence, for Yellowtail, as for many other Apsáalooke, the symbolism of both the wagon wheel and the Ashkísshe reflects the order and relationships found in humankind and in the world.

The correspondence of the ceremonial lodge to the cosmos is a notion shared by the Apsáalooke with the Lakota and many other Plains Indian peoples. In his description of the Sun Dance Lodge, the Lakota elder Black Elk discusses the representations of the Great Spirit, Mother Earth, Four Winds, Spotted Eagle, Sun, Moon, Morning Star, Buffalo, Fire, Water, Rock, and two-legged people in the lodge's structure and explains that

in setting up the sun dance lodge, we are really making the universe in a likeness; for, you see, each of the posts around the lodge represents some particular object of creation, so that the whole circle is the entire creation, and the one tree at the center, upon which the twenty-eight poles rest, is *Wakan-Tanka*, who is the center of everything. Everything comes from Him, and sooner or later everything returns to Him. [Brown 1953:80]

The wagon-wheel image, the specific symbol articulated by Tom Yellowtail, is not itself a pivotal concept that all Apsáalooke, or even all Sun Dance participants, *consciously* acknowledge. Just as various interpretations of the Maker and of medicine mediators pervade the Apsáalooke world, so the term "Ashkísshe" can also refer to the construction of the Sun Dance Lodge in the likeness of a tipi. The lodge in the buffalo days resembled a large tipi, and some see the Big Lodge as an imitation of a tipi lodge. Similarly, Joe

Medicine Crow has suggested that the term *ashammaléaxia* can also mean "Lodges (tipis) are gathered together." The stem *ash* often refers to the noun "lodge" rather than to the verb "to lodge," as indicated by such terms as Ashé Isée (Big Lodge), Ashhilaalíoo (Newly Made Lodge) and Ashkísshe (Imitation Lodge). A consensus on the use of words and images, like a consensus on the nature of the world itself, cannot exist within the framework of the Apsáalooke world view. The paths to the transcendent are many and varied.

Despite the diversity of views and the lack of articulation, except by Yellowtail, the wagon-wheel metaphor pervades throughout the fibers of Apsáalooke society and cosmos. It is an image that helps illuminate the qualities and dynamics of the "driftwood" world view.

## Spoke and Hub: The Structure

In conformity with the wagon-wheel symbolism, the spokes of the wheel should remain distinct. The Apsáalooke envision themselves as unique from the Cheyenne, just as the Cheyenne are unique from non-Indians. Each people has been given its own gifts. Euro-Americans have received the knowledge to perform "surgery," while Indians have acquired the power to "cure diabetes and cancer." Likewise, each individual is recognized for his or her unique attributes, for the gifts that are his or hers alone. These distinctions should be maintained, for the strength of the entire wheel depends on the integrity of each of its parts.

The distinctive nature of religions has been affirmed by the Indian community. When some Catholic clergy tried to "Indianize" the mass, it was not the non-Indian Catholic constituency that objected but the Apsáalooke themselves. The Apsáalooke have acquired an understanding of Catholicism and its rituals and meanings that is fundamentally distinct from their understanding of American Indian religion. As a separate spoke, Catholicism should not be adorned with Sun Dance or Peyote symbols, just as the crucifix should not be placed on the center pole of the Big Lodge. In honoring the Eucharist, the Catholic Apsáalooke hold

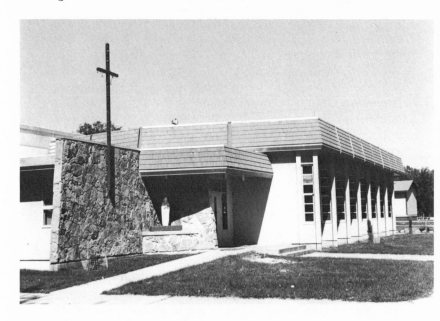

The Roman Catholic Church at Lodge Grass

the Corpus Christi celebration each year and have done so since before the turn of the century. The celebration is a weekend of feasting, processions, prayers, and Communion. When the sponsors of a recent celebration wanted to incorporate Sun Dance songs into the ceremony, the other participants strenuously objected. The songs were not used. Similarly, when a Catholic priest asked if he could use Catholic prayers and rituals during an *áassahke* feast, he was discouraged from doing so. Although an Apsáalooke experiences no conflict by participating in both Sun Dance and Catholic ceremonies and using the language of each, he or she can do so only as long as the two remain distinct.

In a world of many spokes, or separate paths to Akbaatatdía, one can understand more clearly how a multiplicity of interpretations is possible. At a Sun Dance en-

campment a few years ago a story was told of a lost boy who
was taken in and cared for by the Little People. As the rather
detailed account of the adventure came to a close, an elderly
woman perked up, adamantly maintaining that it was not
the Little People but a Buffalo herd that had "adopted" the
boy. Although a few moments of disagreement ensued, con-
tinuing, in fact, a disagreement held during the buffalo days
(Lowie 1918:161–71), both accounts can be accommodated,
and are in fact encouraged, by the Apsáalooke world view.
Just as the Iilápxe can be distinguished from Akbaatatdía,
they can also be an expression of the Maker. The conceptualization of Akbaatatdía itself is also rather varied, as illustrated by the different terms, many reflecting alternate
paths to the transcendent, that are used for the concept.

But, initiated by the same wagon wheel imagery, all
spokes are united by the hub. Consequently, an individual
can partake of Peyote on Saturday, during a meeting of the
Native American Church, and then receive Communion
during a Catholic mass on Sunday without breaking any religious commitments. In fact, many Sun Dance *akbaalía*
are devout Catholics and also "run" Peyote meetings. The
1977 Corpus Christi celebration was organized by Sun
Dance– and Peyote-oriented *akbaalía*.

The cures of the *akbaalía* and the Indian Health Service
physicians are accorded equal respect and potency by the
Apsáalooke. Indian medicine is considered complemen-
tary to, but separate from, Euro-American medicine. The
*akbaalía* are not in competition with their non-Indian
counterparts. Most acknowledge their strengths and weak-
nesses, and when confronted by an affliction that non-
Indian medicine can treat more effectively, they usually advise the patient to see an IHS physician. When rivalries
arise, as they have in the past, they are likely to be caused
by a non-Indian physician's misunderstanding of the role
of the *akbaalía* within Apsáalooke culture. Indeed, the
wife of Tom Yellowtail, Susie, was herself the first Indian
registered nurse in this country. Despite years of admin-

## THE SAME HUB

We'd just sat down at the kitchen table for some coffee when John decided to show me his "peyote things." From a wooden box emerges a fan with rainbow-colored feathers and beaded handle, a similarly beaded wooden staff, and a small brass pillbox. With care, the small container is opened. Revealed is John's "chief peyote button," always cherished, never consumed. "This is who I pray to when someone in my family is sick or in need of something." And then John picks up the small cactus button and turns it over. Glued to the reverse side is a picture of Jesus. For John, whether in an all-night Peyote meeting or a Sunday morning Catholic Mass, the same god is prayed to.*

* For a general overview of the Peyote religion see LaBarre (1969), and for a complete history of the religion as well as a discussion of Apsáalooke peyotism see Stewart (1987).

istering non-Indian medical care, she danced regularly in
the Sun Dance and fully supported her husband's *xapáaliia*
activities.

All religions and all forms of doctoring, though distinct in
their conception of the wheel's hub, are nevertheless bound
by that hub. All are part of the same wheel. All people and
all life forms are interrelated and united by the same ultimate movement. Akbaatatdía permeates creation. During
a vision one realizes this unity of all creation. What one
was necessarily distinct from, one becomes a part of. One
becomes aware of oneness with the Buffalo. Akbaatatdía
speaks through those who receive visions. The visions
establish for the questers a personal relationship with the
Iilápxe and disclose what is implicitly understood but,
under most circumstances, concealed. Whether manifested
in a vision, related in the story of Burnt Face, or addressed
in the prayer given by an *áassahke,* acknowledgment by all
is a transcendent unity that extends to all phenomena.

The wagon-wheel metaphor thus offers a structure that
facilitates for the Apsáalooke an understanding and expression of differentiation and unity in the world.

## The Turning of the Wheel: The Dynamics

The Apsáalooke world is animated and dynamic, alive with
forces and meanings that transcend the human but that
constantly affect and communicate with human beings. In
one sense, humankind is not so much the center as it is
simply one of many spokes in a great wheel. The rhythms
of the world, of the wheel, involve the forces of creation; of
ancestors; of celestial movements; of land, water, plant, and
animal; of the forked tree that reaches into the heavens;
and of humanity itself. Each entity is a necessary spoke
in the wheel. The Apsáalooke are thus receptive to the
life-forces and meanings emanating from all parts of the
world—Rocks, Clouds, Moles, and the Little People all
offer signs and give meanings, all spawn and nurture life.

If an Eagle is sighted in flight by one traveling to a distant place, a hand is raised in the direction of the Eagle,

## THE EAGLE

They're in Joe's four-wheel-drive pickup, out to see some of the country. Open fields and rolling hills are everywhere. To the south, the horizon of the Bighorns is clearly visible. A woodchuck watches from his rocky knoll and then runs off as the pickup nears. They travel on. And then all of a sudden, Joe slams on the brakes and jumps from the cab, pulling the rifle from the rear window rack with him. He aims toward the sky, toward an eagle that circles above. A shot is fired; then a second. But the bird soars out of sight. As Joe later said, "If I was supposed to get it, the Eagle would have allowed itself to be taken."

The Eagle, Déaxkaashe.

and thanks is given, *ahóo*. The Eagle will watch over the traveler, and the traveler will reach his or her destination safely.

Owls, on the other hand, are a sign of potential evil, of trouble, and are to be avoided if at all possible. One family was visited by an Owl that frequented a light pole near its house. The family threw rocks at it and even shot at it, but the Owl remained. Only after the family obtained an Eagle feather specially prepared to ward off the Owl did the ominous visitor depart. One seldom sees a sculpture or a picture of an Owl in an Apsáalooke home.

Like Owls, "ghosts" are also inauspicious signals, omens of possible danger. A Cree family was staying with an Apsáalooke family during the 1977 Crow Fair when they were visited by a "ghost." In the early-morning hours the Cree father had stepped outside the house for a moment, and he saw the form come down the lane toward the river, east of the house. During that same night, while in their camper, the daughter and grandson of the Cree father were visited by the "ghost," who spoke to them in a language they did not understand. The visit was a warning to be heeded. Before the family left for home, the truck and those who had been touched by the "ghost" were smudged with sweet cedar, prayers were said, and sweet sage was placed inside the truck.

Owls and "ghosts," while potentially evil themselves, warn of possible danger so that appropriate action can be taken to ward it off. If one is receptive to the messages of Eagles, Owls, and "ghosts," the world can speak to one, offering meanings.

One afternoon during the 1977 Crow Fair rodeo, a boy fell twice from his horse, but each time his father made him get back on. It was "not the boy's fault"; he could do nothing to prevent the falls. That evening the father obtained medicine for the horse and had prayers said for it. While some said that the boy had fallen "because of the horse" and that anyone who rode the horse would have fallen, others, among them the boy's grandmother, maintained that it was simply the "boy's time to fall." In either case the falls were beyond the immediate control of the boy, no matter how expertly he rode.

When a woman was asked why she would not fasten her seat belt in the car, she said, "If it is my time to go there is nothing I can do about it whether I use a seat belt or not." She was acknowledging linkage to the forces around her.

One December, when the highway was icy, a cow was accidentally killed, hit by a pickup truck unable to stop. The cow's death was a severe financial loss to its owners, even though much of the meat was saved. The loss, however, was greatly tempered by a more significant meaning that emerged from the accident. The grandmother of this family explained that when a family loses a horse or a cow the animal's death is seen as a "substitute" for the death of a human family member. All family members, both human and the animals the family cares for, are intricately connected to forces in a larger web. The cow's death therefore was regarded with some degree of relief.

Each human being is thus seen as part of a larger web of spiritual and human ties rather than as nothing more than an autonomous being, divorced from the influences and consequences of the world. This is not to suggest that the individual is without "choice" and deliberate effect on the world. Individuals are recognized for outstanding (or not-so-outstanding) accomplishments when praise songs are offered on their behalf, and individuals seemingly act on their own volition in vision quests, but in the world of the Apsáalooke, individuals are significantly diffused and submerged within the dynamics and unity of the linkages and personages about them. Each is not self-dependent but, in fact, interdependent with others, including Iilápxe and *áassahke*. The boy who fell from his horse was not so much responsible for the falls as interlinked to a moment in time and a particular horse that initiated the falls. A girl's graduation is not as much the result of her personal abilities as the result of *áassahke* prayers. What constitutes and defines the all-inclusive Apsáalooke world also constitutes and defines the Apsáalooke individual.

But in this world of linkage and animation the inverse is also true: what constitutes and defines the individual also constitutes and defines the world. To appreciate this understanding, the role and significance of human participation in the cosmos must be reappraised. To illustrate the character of this involvement, oral language must be considered.

Spoken words are not just semantic means of communication or descriptions of phenomena. They are also endowed with power that can affect the context in which they are expressed. In fact, words can bring about phenomena (Frey 1983). Telling a story, singing a song, and holding a conversation are certainly as physically manifest and active as any public act. But the story, the song, the dialogue, and, specifically, the words and symbols of which they are composed are also inundated with creative power.

A similar notion exists among the Navajo. Sam Gill (1977) has demonstrated the "performative force" of Navajo prayer acts, showing that the structure of prayer is that of a "person," specifically a deity. The prayer is the embodiment of the deity and is as animated and as omnipotent as the particular deity it conveys. Thus on each occasion of ceremonial prayer, such as when the sick are doctored, the world is directly influenced by the particular deity of the prayer.

While the Apsáalooke do not view a prayer, a story, a song, or a word as a deity, they do conceive of language as an active agent. Words, in whatever form they are expressed, have the power to affect an environment; words are as "real as a rock."

Among the Apsáalooke one does not talk "too much" about illness. An explanation for this understanding lies in the term *dasshússuua*, literally meaning "breaking with the mouth." Words, brought forth through the mouth, have the ability to break, to alter or to bring about, a situation. One may hesitate to discuss an illness, fearing that the use of words describing it may inadvertently cause the affliction. In the same vein, one does not say, "Good-bye," after a visit. Rather, one says, "See you later," or, in Apsáalooke, "diiawákaawik." The Apsáalooke say that "good-bye is too final." Saying it could cause those involved never to see each other again, a "breaking with the mouth."

Words cannot be used inappropriately without harmful consequences. One should always be deliberate in the manner in which one uses words. If a public vow is made to sponsor a Sun Dance and the vow is not fulfilled, some sort of negative action will affect the one who made the vow. It is easy to comprehend why all public praise of another should be expressed by an older man who is experienced in the proper use of words or by someone who has the "right" to speak publicly, who has medicine pertaining to the proper use of words. Otherwise the potential for serious harm exists.

But using words properly can bring great benefit. When an Indian name is bestowed, and the name "agrees with the child," the name may bring about whatever it describes. The Sunrise song of the Sun Dance helps the dancers attain their desired union with the morning Sun, to communicate with it and receive a vision.

When a story is told before a group of eager listeners, it is not told simply to entertain or to illustrate a character or an event. As adventures are portrayed in words, the words

## CURTAIN BOY AND SPRING BOY

Several are gathered around as the storyteller begins.

"There's a young man and woman living alone in the mountains. They're married and care for each other very much. Each day he goes out and hunts the deer, and brings back meat and hides for this wife to prepare. Each day she gathers berries and makes the clothes for the two of them. They care for each other very much.

"One day when the husband is out hunting, an old woman comes into camp . . ."

Some are familiar enough with the account to anticipate its course. Yet all will undergo the adventure as if for the first time. A tear is shed, now a laugh is heard as the story's landscape is entered into. The listeners become the characters in the story. Anticipation is replaced with participation.

The teller is a master. The tale is embellished with so much texture, detail, and repetition that any hope of extracting a coherent and singular plot is impossible. Hands and intonation oscillate, highlighting this or that part of the unfolding story. The words flow with a deliberateness, and long pauses augment seemingly every other sentence. The pauses are not silent though. This or that listener responds with a firm *ée* (yes), acknowledging his involvement in the adventure. A storyteller knows that when the listeners grow silent, the story is to end, for there are no longer any participants. And being a master teller, the storyteller remembers the account of Curtain Boy and Spring Boy well, having shared it countless times before.

But as the story unfolds, the storyteller soon realizes the volition it has. He speaks the words yet is as a listener to them. Curtain Boy and Spring Boy are released, becoming the real tellers of the story. They set the pace, offer the word order, and every once in a while reveal something of the story not even remembered by the storyteller.

"The old woman walks with a limp and a cane. She wears ragged clothes and has an ugly face. She's not pleasant to look at. The young woman immediately offers her some food. But the old woman refuses it. Again food is offered, this time the best the young couple has. Still it is refused. 'I want to eat my meal on the belly of a pregnant woman.' Being generous, the young woman lies down, pulls up her dress and serves the meal on her huge belly. After consuming all the food, the old woman pulls out her knife and kills the mother, cutting open her belly and throwing the babies away. One boy is thrown inside the tipi, behind the liner of the lodge; the other boy is thrown into a nearby spring. The old woman sets the body of the young woman up against the lodge and with a hot coal burns a smile into her face. She then leaves.

"Later that day the husband returns and sees his wife busy, mending something perhaps. He feels good seeing the smile she has for him. But as he gets closer, he senses something wrong. She's usually up, running toward him. And then he sees! How could this be?"

"He places her body along with her best things in a scaffolding not far from the lodge. He cuts his braids and skin, letting the blood flow freely. He just sits there day after day.

"One day he hears something coming from inside the tipi. 'Feed me Father, feed me. I'm hungry.' He goes in and looks around. 'Feed me.' From behind the liner he pulls out a small boy. 'Feed me, Father.' The father feeds his sons, who tell him what happened to their mother. 'An old woman came into camp and insisted on eating off our mother's belly. When she finished, she did this to us.'

"The young man's sorrow is soon replaced with his joy for his sons, Curtain Boy and Spring Boy. Each day he teaches them the lessons of growing up. He cares for them very much. See them there?" *

* This account continues below with three of Curtain Boy and Spring Boy's adventures.

create the adventures portrayed. The story comes alive, and the listeners are not passive recipients, but active participants, in the story.

To listen to an Apsáalooke story is to experience the story. After a man returned from an extended tour of Europe, where he had seen endless wonders, he began early one evening to relate in detail, as a storyteller, his experiences to his family. By the early-morning hours, as many were dozing off and few were offering "Ée," the listeners were still waiting to board the ship for Europe. Every detail of the journey to New York first had to be related, brought to life, and participated in by the listeners.

Not only oral language but all other forms of Apsáalooke symbolic expression are inundated with creative power. The categorical distinction between a story, a song, a beaded belt, an architectural structure, and an overt human action is minimal. All are animated, and all affect that with which they are in proximity. The particular floral design and colors beaded into a Sun Dancer's belt by his grandmother provide the dancer with a refreshing wrap for his body. When the objects from a medicine bundle are smudged in sweet-cedar incense and placed symmetrically on an elk hide during the bundle opening, their placement offers a channel for a prayer or a cure. Inside one of the several hundred tipis at the Crow Fair encampment, an Apsáalooke looks up through the smoke flaps. The architectural form that envelops him—a circle of canvas and lodgepole pine planted in the earth and extended into the sky—reiterates a sense of place within the cosmos. The tipi becomes a home within a home.

As *baaxpée* emanates from Akbaatatdía, and as Akbaatatdía permeates all phenomena, so *baaxpée* flows from each of the Maker's expressions, not only from the Iilápxe but also from the Apsáalooke. *Baaxpée* flows from words, from songs, from art, and from architecture. Not only does the wagon wheel encompass and link together all its spokes, but the hub of this great wheel is necessarily in all entities, a pervasive center, a source of animation and meaning

Words of wisdom, words of power are shared by Susie Yellowtail as
she relates a story.

shared within all. The human, in this sense, is not only a
"spoke" but also a "hub," a center of the great wheel. The
world animated by meaning and life-giving force in which
the Apsáalooke reciprocate with and interdepend on others
is, in fact, a world animated and made meaningful by the
Apsáalooke act of participating in it. Perhaps this is the ultimate expression of reciprocity. The Apsáalooke and the
world are extensions of each other. Neither the cosmos nor
the human beings can be autonomous. Interdependence,
reciprocity, animation, and transcendence vibrate equally
from and throughout the Apsáalooke and their world.

Oral literature offers the Apsáalooke a model for this ani-
mating behavior. The story of Curtain Boy and Spring Boy
exemplifies the transformative relationship that the Apsáalooke can enter into with the world. Curtain Boy and
Spring Boy, with only their skill and daring to aid them,
challenge and overcome a series of formidable adversaries.

## THE ADVENTURES CONTINUE

The boys are gathered around as their father explains, "Stay away from that ridge over there. There's a huge tree, and if you walk by, it'll come crashing down on you. It's dangerous! Stay away." So the boys say, "Let's go," and are off.

The boys are running, chasing each other as they approach the tree. It sees them. Carefree and faster they run toward the giant tree. Just as they are about to run under it, they stop and the tree comes crashing down. Quickly they are on top of it, breaking off the tree's branches. It stays down for good now.

Curtain Boy and Spring Boy bring back to their father some of the tree's branches. "You boys are crazy!"

The boys are gathered around as their father tells them to "stay away from that valley over there. Roaming in it is a great buffalo. It's so large that it can swallow you up just like that. Stay away; it's dangerous!" The boys say, "Let's go," and are off.

As they travel to the valley, they cut down some stout saplings and tie them to their backs. There it is. It's huge. Running this way, then that, they get close. The buffalo opens his mouth and simply inhales the boys. Inside the great belly, the boys can see some decomposed people, some half-decomposed people, and some people who must have recently been inhaled, for they are sitting over to the side, talking. Curtain Boy yells out to the buffalo, asking if it would be all right to put on a Sun Dance, right inside the belly. Well, the buffalo thinks that's a grand idea, after all, he's never had a Sun Dance held inside himself before. With the saplings, the boys build the lodge. Part of the belly wall makes a fine drum, and pretty soon everyone who can is up dancing. Spring Boy then climbs to the top of the lodge and with his knife begins poking around here and there. "Stop that, what are you doing?" the buffalo shouts. And there it is, what Spring Boy is looking for. It's beating away. With a tremendous jab the knife pierces the heart of the buffalo. A flood of blood flows forth, and everyone is washed out through the buffalo's mouth. There it is wallowing and kicking about on its side. Then it's still. The boys cut off its tongue and give it to their father. "You boys are crazy!"

The boys are gathered around and their father tells them to "stay away from the camp of the snakes. They're dangerous; their noses are so sharp that they can burrow into the ground, travel like lightning, and come up wherever they please. And they don't warn you before they strike. Stay away; it's dangerous!" So the boys say, "Let's go," and are off.

As they travel to the snake's camp, the boys place flat stones in their breechcloths. Coming upon the camp, the boys go into the lodge and sit down. A few of the snakes immediately go into the ground and try to attack the boys. But when they come up, they bang their heads against the flat rocks and can't get inside their guests. The chief of the snakes asks, "What are you doing here? We seldom get visitors." "We've come to tell you some stories." "That sounds good. No one has ever done that before. Go ahead boys."

So the boys start in.

"We're out hunting deer. It's winter, and the tracks are clear, but the snow is so deep that each step becomes more difficult. Having gotten the deer and loading the heavy load on our backs, the trip home through this deep snow is even more tiring. It is so wonderful to finally get back to camp, start up a warm fire, and cook the fresh meat. And we fall fast asleep.

"The spring thaw is on and thick mud and water is everywhere. It's time to move camp. It's a dirty job packing up. When we finally get going, we travel all day long and all the next day, and the next. The streams and rivers are swollen with fast waters and are very difficult to cross. Exhausted by the long journey, it's so nice to finally gather around the fire of the lodge, with warm and soft buffalo robes on, and fall fast asleep."

And pretty soon all the snakes are asleep as well! So the boys take out their knives and one by one, cut off the head of the snakes. Just as they are about to finish the job, the last snake, the chief snake, wakes up and dives into the ground. And when he comes up, he comes up in Spring Boy's leg. So Curtain Boy cuts off the leg to get the snake out, but it's gone into the thigh. So Curtain Boy cuts off the thigh, but it's gone into the belly of Spring Boy. So the belly is cut open, but the snake has gone into the chest. So Curtain Boy cuts open the chest, but finds the snake gone, gone into the head. So Curtain Boy cuts off the head of his brother and sets it over a fire to boil out the snake. And sure enough, the snake comes out. Holding him tight, Curtain Boy is just about to cut off the snakes head when it asks for its life. "I'll never strike again without first warning you. I'll put rattles on my tail. Let me go!" And just to make sure the snake can't sneak up on you, Curtain Boy scrapes the head of that snake against his breechcloth stone. The snake's head becomes as flat as the stone.

But poor Spring Boy is in a bad way. So Curtain Boy builds a sweat bath, heats up the rocks, and takes a sweat with all the parts of his brother. When the door flap is finally raised, out of the steam come Curtain Boy and Spring Boy. With the heads of some of the snakes, the boys return home to their father. "You boys are crazy!" *

*These three segments of the rather lengthy cycle of Curtain Boy and Spring Boy adventures were told to me with a considerable degree of embellishment. The informant's account nevertheless retained amazingly close parallels to the cycle as first recorded by Lowie (1918:74–98).

The world is transformed and made a safer place in which to travel.

In direct contrast to the story of Curtain Boy and Spring Boy is the account of Burnt Face, discussed earlier. While Curtain Boy is assertive and creative, challenging his adversaries and transforming his world, Burnt Face is receptive and dependent, seeking out a paternal bond and, once he acquires it, depending upon it. Both sets of stories serve as models by which the Apsáalooke can better express and understand the complexities of their world.

The oral literature and the wagon-wheel metaphor thus offer a dynamics that facilitates for the Apsáalooke an understanding and expression of receptivity and dependence as well as of creativity and animation in the world.

### Driftwood and Wagon Wheel: Conclusion

The Apsáalooke world is indeed a great wheel in which all entities—land, animal, spirit, and human—are necessarily and simultaneously both "spoke," expressive of diversity and the uniqueness of each phenomenon, and "hub," expressive of the unity of all phenomena. And as in a great wheel, all entities are necessarily both "spoke," and therefore receptive to and interdependent on the totality of the wheel, and "hub," and therefore the source of meaning and life-force in the wheel. The Iilápxe and Akbaatatdía can be conceptualized as fundamentally differentiated, as many Apsáalooke do, or as essentially expressive of the same spiritual essence, as others insist. While questing on a butte or in the Big Lodge, a faster distinguishes his or her ultimate uniqueness by offering sincerity so that he or she will be accepted into union with Akbaatatdía. The faster and the Buffalo become a single expression during the vision. Similarly, because each Apsáalooke is both "spoke" and "hub," each can listen for the Eagle's cry and receive its message as well as become the Eagle and soar high among the clouds. An Apsáalooke can depend on the power of a name given by an *áassahke* as well as speak the name of an illness and cause it to occur. As an *akbaalía* is directed by the Iilápxe, he also directs *baaxpée* into patients by using the feathers of the Eagle. During the telling of a story, a listener can become the receptive and dependent Burnt Face or the creative and assertive Curtain Boy or Old Man Coyote. And once one of the stories is told, one can carry forth and manifest the imagery of Burnt Face or of Old Man Coyote while questing in the Sun Dance Lodge or while deceiving a gatekeeper at the Crow Fair rodeo.

While an Iilápxe, a faster, and any other being can be considered distinct from Akbaatatdía, each endowed with particular attributes and characteristics, each receptive to and interdependent with Akbaatatdía for meaning and life, all can also be considered as one, a unity of expression and dynamics, the source of creativity and meaning.

With this in mind one can better appreciate the dynamic and, in a sense, deliberate and sovereign role that the individual plays in the Apsáalooke world. Because the world is not conceptualized as passive, neither is the individual. Both are active agents. Although as a "spoke," an individual interdepends with the animated world, the interdependence is not deterministic. Each individual is linked to and influenced by a world alive with meaning and force, but this linkage does not predetermine one's fate. One can be receptive to the messages of the Eagle or look away; one can enter the Big Lodge or choose not to "blow the whistle"; one can heed the warnings of the Owl or ignore them. The father of the boy who fell off his horse decided to obtain medicine for the horse to prevent the boy from falling again during the race. The boy's grandmother would perhaps have chosen differently. A choice is made. A consequence awaits. As a "hub" each individual acts upon the world, choosing a course of action, and creating a path. The very words one chooses help to bring the path about. Medicine can be directed to cure or "to take the arm." A name can nurture or cripple. As a story is being told, a listener can become part of Burnt Face's adventure or elect not to listen. A choice is made. A consequence awaits.

Several years ago, while walking alone in the mountains,

an old man was met by the Little People. He was taken to the mouth of a great cave, where the Little People asked him to choose between two tunnels. One went but a short distance; the other seemed endless. The choice was between two religious paths. The man chose the tunnel without end, the Sun Dance religion. As an *akbaalía,* the man has brought the Sun Dance to those in need, creating a path that he and others could follow. As Old Man Coyote first traveled with the Sun from east to west, mapping out the landscape and bringing forth the creation, so each Apsáalooke can continue to do so.

Yellowtail's image of the world as a great wagon wheel thus not only expresses the qualities inherent in "as driftwood lodges" but also conveys a sense of the dynamics of that world view. The interchange between spoke and hub in all entities and throughout the cosmos, and the symbolism of diversity and unity, receptivity and creativity, and dependence and volition intrinsic to the wagon wheel are paralleled in the structure and dynamics of the "driftwood" metaphor. The spoke is to the individual pieces of driftwood as the hub is to the lodging of the driftwood. Each Apsáalooke is like a piece of driftwood, receptive, interlinked, and dependent, yet each is also like a linkage to the others about him or her, creating and assuring the unity of the entire bundle.

While the wagon wheel perhaps expresses the idea more precisely, both images refer to the identical dynamics transpiring in the various levels of the Apsáalooke world. Both the driftwood and the wagon-wheel images refer to the immediate and concrete world of social relations, human and natural adversaries, and human and spiritual kinfolk, where the *body* of the Apsáalooke is nurtured. Both images also refer to the transcendent world of spiritual attainment, questing and receptivity, and visions and creativity, where the *soul* of the Apsáalooke is nurtured. Finally, because of the inevitable dilemmas encountered by differentiation versus oneness and by receptivity and dependence versus creativity and volition, both the driftwood and the wagon-

The Big Lodge one year after the Sun Dance.

wheel images refer to the philosophical and existential worlds, where those dilemmas are expressed and mediated, and where the *consciousness* of the Apsáalooke is nurtured.

N. Scott Momaday, the Pulitzer Prize–winning Kiowa poet and scholar, once commented: "What we are is what we imagine. Our very existence consists in our imagination of ourselves. Our best destiny is to imagine, at least, completely, who and what, and *that* we are. The greatest tragedy that can befall us is to go unimagined" (1983:48). The Apsáalooke are, in fact, what they have imagined themselves to be. The imagery of driftwood lodging along the bank of a turbulent river, expressed through such configurations as *áassahke, xapáaliia,* and the turning of the wagon wheel, has contributed to the continued vitality of

the Apsáalooke. As the Apsáalooke encounter adversity and
opponents, both subtle and overt, at every bend, they will
cling together and depend on each other, son and daughter
with *áassahke* and Iilápxe, each as both spoke and hub.
This image has offered the Apsáalooke a means for successfully challenging the tremendous pressures of assimilation
that they have encountered throughout their history. And
the driftwood continues to lodge.

It is fitting that this journey into the Apsáalooke world
began with an image of driftwood and ends with one of
a wagon wheel. As the journey has moved from the confu-
sion and turbulence of driftwood in a river to the certainty
and regularity of pattern in a wagon wheel, I hope a similar
movement has occurred in the reader's journey of understanding the world of the Apsáalooke.

# Concept of World View

WORLD VIEW REFERS TO the symbolic categories and processes that help a given people interpret the world about them and generate their behavior. A world view is the cognitive and affective system that organizes both a conceptualization and an expression of time, space, being, and causation. World view not only reflects the way the world is conceived, passively describing it, but also contributes to the conceiving of that world, actively helping bring it about.

It is critical that the conceptual tool used in framing the Apsáalooke materials is consistent with what it is framing. While my use of the concept of world view largely conforms to its use by other anthropologists, a deviation does exist.[1] Most applications of the concept implicitly, if not explicitly, suggest that world view is epiphenomenal to the material conditions of a society. The social and economic institutions, for instance, are considered primary and mold the infrastructure about them, including the world view. In his monumental work *The Tewa World* (1969), Alfonso Ortiz takes exception to this position. He demonstrates that in Pueblo Indian society the relationship between the social institutions and world view is one of dynamics and feedback; the world view not only reflects the social order but gives it "direction and continuity as well" (1969:4).

While my concern is not with the relationship between

---

[1] See Kearney (1975) for a review of the pertinent literature on the concept of world view.

certain social institutions and world view, as it was for Ortiz, I am interested in the relationship between the praxis and material levels of experience and the world view. In this relationship a dynamics also predominates. I am not suggesting, for instance, that the world-view imagery associated with *ashammaléaxia* and with the clan structure is derived from those social relations and then imparted throughout the entire Apsáalooke world. Rather, the clan structure as well as the other social institutions discussed in this book are equally influenced by, and in turn influence, the Apsáalooke world view. It is, after all, held by the Apsáalooke that the clan institution was created by Old Man Coyote or, rephrased, that the social order was derived from the spiritual order. The Apsáalooke vision of the material world as epiphenomenal to the transcendent world can be accommodated much more easily in a concept of world view that acknowledges such a dynamics.

The concept of world view is consequently given an active, rather than simply a passive, significance. In the instance of the Apsáalooke, this is particularly relevant in observing the creative role played by human participation in the world. While a world view is influenced by and reflects much of the social order, human social actions, as carriers of a world view, are also orchestrated by that world view. In the Apsáalooke world, spiritual creative forces act not only through the natural world but through human beings as well; human beings are not simply acted upon by the spiritual. The spiritual acts through them as well, and thus they affect the world about them. The world is, in part, brought about by the human act of participating in it. As a dynamics resides in the various levels of the Apsáalooke portrait, so too a dynamics must reside in the conceptual levels of the frame for that portrait.

While much of the contemporary Apsáalooke world view is characterized as oriented to *ashammaléaxia* (as driftwood lodges), the Apsáalooke can also participate in world views involving qualities quite distinct from those discussed here. Such views may envision a world inhabited by turbulent currents and adversaries at *every* bend, in which individuals are self-focused tricksters, duping others before they themselves are duped. There is no unified, integrated, and consistent world view encompassing Apsáalooke society. Rather, there is a matrix of varied views. I find Clifford Geertz's image of cultural organization as an "octopoid" system most applicable in conceptualizing the world view of the Apsáalooke or, for that matter, of any people (1973:408). If I may borrow Geertz's analogy, world view is rather like an octopus, with multiple tentacles neurally integrated only loosely with each other and with the brain, but maintaining its viability nonetheless, and moving about and surviving, however cumbersome it may be. A world view encompasses views of the world that are often disjointed from, and occasionally contradictory to, each other. Although it describes but a single thrust of the entire Apsáalooke world view, even the "driftwood" view of the world oscillates with a multiplicity of possible perspectives.

By extension, because the "driftwood" world view does not encompass the entire Apsáalooke society, and because the *áassahke* and *xapáaliia* institutions are expressions of that world view, they necessarily are not participated in by the entire Apsáalooke population. While both institutions have demonstrated an amazing resilience through time, a unanimity toward them has not. The influence of Euro-American assimilation has diverted some Apsáalooke away from their traditional institutions. Although the *áassahke* and *xapáaliia* institutions are indeed pivotal for most Apsáalooke, the "driftwood" world view is not shared by all Apsáalooke, and thus neither are these two institutions.

# Pronunciation Key and Glossary

| Vowels | Pronunciation |
|---|---|
| a | sof<u>a</u> |
| u | p<u>u</u>t |
| i | p<u>i</u>t |
| o | m<u>o</u>tor |
| aa | f<u>a</u>ther |
| uu | d<u>o</u> |
| ii | k<u>e</u>y |
| ee | <u>a</u>ble |
| oo | <u>o</u>wn |
| ua | kul<u>ua</u> |
| ia | ar<u>ea</u> |
| e | t<u>a</u>ke |
| e | c<u>a</u>t (when at word ending) |

| Consonants | |
|---|---|
| b | <u>b</u>e |
| d | <u>d</u>id |
| h | <u>h</u>e |
| m | <u>m</u>an |
| n | <u>n</u>ame |
| w | <u>w</u>e |
| l | <u>l</u>ife |
| x | <u>acht</u> (German ch) |
| s | <u>s</u>tone |
| s | <u>z</u>one (occurring between vowels) |
| ch | <u>ch</u>ild |
| ch | <u>j</u>oke (occurring between vowels) |
| p | <u>p</u>ound |

| p | <u>b</u>aby (occurring between vowels) |
|---|---|
| sh | <u>sh</u>e |
| sh | vi<u>s</u>ion (occurring between vowels) |
| t | <u>t</u>ime |
| t | <u>d</u>eed (occurring between vowels) |
| k | <u>k</u>in |
| k | <u>g</u>ood (occurring between vowels) |

Phonetic values are derived from those used in the Crow Agency and Wyola Bilingual Education programs.

*Accent*

Each Apsáalooke word has a vowel that is stressed when the word is pronounced. The stressed vowel is indicated by an accent placed directly above it.

**Glossary**

*áannutche.* To curse someone, to use bad medicine, "to take the arm."

*áassahke.* My clan uncle and aunt (generic term of reference).

*ahóo.* Thanks.

*akbaalía.* A doctor, a medicine man, "one who doctors."

Akbaatatdía. The Maker, "the One Who Has Made Everything."

*akéeleete.* Orphan, "one with no possessions, one who has nothing."

*ammaakalátche.* Belief, "what he or she believes."

*ammaakée.* Giveaway.

announcer. A camp crier, one who speaks publicly for another.

Apsáalooke. Crow people, "children of the large-beaked bird."

*ashammaléaxia.* Clan, "as driftwood lodges."

*ashhéeleetaawaalissuua.* Ceremonial dance-parade involving giveaways held on the last day of Crow Fair.

Ashé Isée. Big Lodge.

Ashhilaalíoo. Newly Made Lodge clan.

Ashííooshe. Sore Lip clan.

Ashkáamne. Piegan clan.

Ashképkawiia. Bad War Deeds clan.

Ashkísshe. Sun Dance, "imitation lodge."

Ashshitchíte. Big Lodge clan.

Awakkulé. Dwarf, "Little People."

*awúshbileele.* Act of sweat bathing, "he or she went into the sweat lodge."

*áxxaashe.* Sun.

*axée, axéekaate.* "My father" (male speaker, term of address).

*baaattaakúuo.* To make a vow, or a pledge or to desire good luck or a good blessing for another person.

*baachichíilik.* Seeking assistance or a vision during a fast, "he or she is looking for something."

*baakáate.* My child (generic term).

Báakukkule. The One Above.

*baalía.* To cure, "to doctor."

*baashchíile.* White person, "person with yellow eyes."

*baaúuwatshiile.* Meadowlark.

*baaxpáak.* Person with *baaxpée,* "he or she has *baaxpée.*"

*baaxpée.* Power transcending the ordinary, something mysterious or spiritual, good luck.

*bachéem.* A man.

*bachuuké.* "My younger brother" (male and female speaker).

bad medicine. To use *xapáaliia* to injure another.

*balasáhte.* Forked tree.

*basaakáa.* "My father" (female speaker, term of address).

*basáake.* "My father," clan uncle (female speaker, term of reference).

Big Lodge. Sun Dance structure.

*biiké.* "My older brother" (male speaker).

*biilápxe.* "My father," clan uncle (male speaker, term of reference).

*biiwaatcheeshkáatak.* I am poor, pitiful.

Bilikóoshe. Whistling Water clan.

*bilisshíissannee.* "to fast from water" (and food).

*bisaalé.* "My older brother" (female speaker).

*bishée.* Buffalo.

blow or use the whistle. To participate in the Sun Dance.

*chiwakíia.* To pray, "to ask repeatedly."

danced hard. Participated with vigor and sincerity.

*dasshússuua.* "Breaking with the mouth."

*déaxkaashe.* Eagle.

*díakaashe.* He or she did it with determination, with effort, with pride or with sincerity, "he or she really did it."

*diiawákaawik.* See you later (when one is speaking to another person).

*dissúua.* "To dance."

dry up. To fast and sacrifice during a Sun Dance.

*ée.* Yes.

fast. Abstain from food and water as during a Sun Dance or a vision quest.

*hawassée.* "To cure."

*iichíilikaashe.* Elk.

Iichíkbaalee. "The First Doer."

Iilápxe. Medicine mediator, "my Father."

Isáahke. Old Man.

Isáahkawuattee. Old Man Coyote.

making medicine. Using *baaxpée.*

put on or up. To sponsor a ceremony.

run. To coordinate and officiate over a ceremony.

*suuwassée.* First spring thunder, "first thunder."

sweat. A ritual of prayer and purification conducted in a steam lodge.

touch up. Apply *baaxpée* with Eagle feathers, as during a curing ceremony.

Úuwuutasshe. Greasy Mouth clan

*xapáalialustuua.* Opening of the medicine bundles.

*xapáaliia.* Medicine bundle, tangible image of *baaxpée.*

Xúhkaalaxche. Ties-in-a-Bundle clan.

# Bibliography

## Apsáalooke Materials

Bradley, Charles C., Jr. 1970. After the Buffalo Days: Documents on Crow Indians from the 1880s to the 1920s. Master's thesis, Montana State University, Bozeman.

————. 1982. The Effect of Abundant Resources on the History of the Crow Reservation Schools. Ed.D. diss., Montana State University, Bozeman.

Brooke, William. 1981. Yellowtail Dam: A Study in Indian Land. Honors thesis, Carroll College, Helena, Mont.

Brown, Mark. 1961. *Plainsmen of the Yellowstone*. Lincoln: University of Nebraska Press, Bison Books.

Calloway, Colin. 1986. Sword Bearer and the "Crow Outbreak," 1887. *Montana, the Magazine of Western History* 36, no. 4:38–51.

Catlin, George. 1973. *Letters and Notes on the Manners, Customs and Condition of the North American Indians*. New York: Dover. Originally published in 1844.

Curtis, Edward. 1970. *The North American Indian*, Vol. 4, *The Apsaroke, or Crows*. New York: Johnson Reprint. Originally published in 1909.

Davis, Leslie, ed. 1979. Symposium on the Crow-Hidatsa Separation. *Archeology in Montana* 20, no. 3 (entire issue).

Denig, Edwin Thompson. 1961. "On the Crow Nation." In John Ewers, ed. *Five Tribes of the Upper Missouri: Sioux, Arickaras, Assiniboines, Crees, Crows*. Norman: University of Oklahoma Press. Originally published in 1953.

Eggan, Fred. 1955. "The Cheyenne and Arapaho Kinship System." In Fred Eggan, ed. *Social Organization of the North American Tribes.* Enlarged edition. Chicago: University of Chicago Press.

Ehrlich, Clara. 1937. Tribal Culture in Crow Mythology. *Journal of American Folklore* 50, no. 198:307–408.

Fitzgerald, Michael O., ed. Forthcoming. *Yellowtail: The Medicine Man and Sun Dance Chief Speaks of the Sacred Ways of the Crow.*

Frey, Rodney. 1979. To Dance Together: Ethnography in Apsáalooke (Crow) Culture. Ph.D. diss., University of Colorado, Boulder.

————. 1983. Re-Telling One's Own: Storytelling Among the Apsáalooke (Crow Indians). *Plains Anthropologist* 28:129–35.

Frison, George. 1967. Archaeological Evidence of the Crow Indians in Northern Wyoming: A Study of Late Prehistoric Period Buffalo Economy. Ph.D. diss., University of Michigan, Ann Arbor.

————. 1979. The Crow Indian Occupation of the High Plains: Archeological Evidence. *Archeology in Montana* 20, no. 3:3–16.

Graczsk, Randolph, Fr. 1975. The Sweat Lodge. *Close-Up* April.

Hathaway, Flora. 1970. *Old Man Coyote: Crow Legends of Creation.* Billings: Montana Reading Publications.

Heidenreich, C. Adrian. 1971. Ethnodocumentary of the Crow Indians of Montana, 1824–1862. Ph.D. diss., University of Oregon, Eugene.

————. 1976. The Persistence of Values Among the Crow Indians. Paper read at symposium, 1976 American Anthropological Association Meetings, Washington, D.C.

————. 1979. The Bearing of Ethnohistoric Data on the Crow-Hidatsa Separation(s). *Archeology in Montana* 20, no. 3:87–111.

————. 1981. The Crow Indian Delegation to Washington, D.C., in 1880. *Montana, the Magazine of Western History* 31, no. 2:54–67.

————. 1985. The Native American's Yellowstone. *Montana, the Magazine of Western History* 35, no. 4:2–17.

Linderman, Frank. 1962. *Plenty-coups, Chief of the Crows.* Lincoln: University of Nebraska Press, Bison Books. Originally published in 1930.

————. 1974. *Pretty-shield, Medicine Woman of the Crows.* Lincoln: University of Nebraska Press, Bison Books. Originally published in 1932.

Lowie, Robert. 1912. Social Life of the Crow Indians. *Anthropological Papers of the American Museum of Natural History* 9:181–247. Reprint, New York: AMS Reprint.

———. 1913. Societies of the Crow, Hidatsa and Mandan Indians. *Anthropological Papers of the American Museum of Natural History* 11:45–358.

———. 1915. The Sun Dance of the Crow Indians. *Anthropological Papers of the American Museum of Natural History* 16:1–50. Reprint, New York: AMS Reprint.

———. 1917. Notes on the Social Organization and Custom of the Mandan, Hidatsa and Crow Indians. *Anthropological Papers of the American Museum of Natural History.* 21:3–99. Reprint, New York: AMS Reprint.

———. 1918. Myths and Traditions of the Crow Indians. *Anthropological Papers of the American Museum of Natural History.* 25:1–308. Reprint, New York: AMS Reprint.

———. 1919. The Tobacco Society of the Crow Indians. *Anthropological Papers of the American Museum of Natural History* 21:101–200. Reprint, New York: AMS Reprint.

———. 1922a. The Material Culture of the Crow Indians. *Anthropological Papers of the American Museum of Natural History* 21:201–70. Reprint, New York: AMS Reprint.

———. 1922b. Crow Indian Art. *Anthropological Papers of the American Museum of Natural History* 21:271–322.

———. 1922c. The Religion of the Crow Indians. *Anthropological Papers of the American Museum of Natural History* 25:311–444. Reprint, New York: AMS Reprint.

———. 1924. Minor Ceremonies of the Crow Indians. *Anthropological Papers of the American Museum of Natural History* 21:323–365.

———. 1970. *Primitive Religion.* New York: Liveright. Originally published in 1948.

———. 1983. *The Crow Indians.* Lincoln: University of Nebraska Press, Bison Books. Originally published in 1935.

Marquis, Thomas B. 1974. *Memoirs of a White Crow Indian (Thomas H. Leforge).* Lincoln: University of Nebraska Press, Bison Books. Originally published in 1928.

Matthews, G. Hubert. 1976. Bilingual Education at Crow Agency. *Studies in Language Learning* 1:265–89.

————. 1977. Personal communications.

————. 1979. Glottochronology and the Separation of the Crow and Hidatsa. *Archeology in Montana* 20, no. 3:113–25.

Medicine Crow, Joe. 1939. The Effects of European Culture Contacts upon the Economic, Social, and Religious Life of Crow Indians. Master's thesis, University of Southern California, Los Angeles.

————. 1979a. The Crow Migration Story. *Archeology in Montana* 20, no. 3:63–72.

————. 1979b. *Medicine Crow.* Crow Agency: Crow Central Education Commission.

Medicine Crow, Joe, and Charles Bradley, Jr. 1976. *The Crow Indians: 100 Years of Acculturation.* Wyola, Mont.: Wyola Bilingual Project.

Nabokov, Peter. 1967. *Two Leggings: The Making of a Crow Warrior.* New York: Crowell.

Old Coyote, Henry. 1974. *Crow Indian Child Raising.* Crow Agency, Mont.: Crow Agency Bilingual Education.

Oliver, Symmes E. 1962. Ecology and Cultural Continuity as Contributing Factors in the Social Organization of the Plains Indians. *University of California Publications in American Archaeology and Ethnology* 48, no. 1 (Berkeley).

Oswalt, Wendell H. 1978. The Crow: Plains Warriors and Bison Hunters. In *This Land Was Theirs.* New York: Random House.

*Pryor Clan History.* 1973. Mimeographed.

Reed, John. 1976. A Survey of Bilingualism Among Crow Indian Students. Mimeographed.

————. 1978. A Sociolinguistic Study of Crow Language Maintenance. Ph.D. diss., University of New Mexico, Albuquerque.

Simms, S.C. 1903a. *Traditions of the Crows.* Field Columbian Museum, publication no. 85. Anthropological Series, Vol. 2, no. 6, Chicago.

————. 1903b. A Wheel–shaped Stone Monument in Wyoming. *American Anthropologist*, n.s. 5:107–10.

Smith, Burton. 1986. Politics and the Crow Indian Land Cessions. *Montana, the Magazine of Western History* 36, no. 4:24–37.

Spier, Leslie. 1921. The Sun Dance of the Plains Indians: Its Development and Diffusion. *Anthropological Papers of the American Museum of Natural History* 16:451–527.

Stafford, John W. 1972. Crow Culture Change. Ph.D. diss., Michigan State University, East Lansing.

Stewart, Omer. 1987. *Peyote Religion: A History.* Norman: University of Oklahoma Press.

Voget, Fred. 1948. Individual Motivation in the Diffusion of the Wind River Shoshone Sun Dance to the Crow Indians. *American Anthropologist* 50:634–46.

————. 1964. Warfare and the Integration of Crow Indian Culture. In Ward Goodenenough, ed. *Explorations in Cultural Anthropology: Essays in Honor of George Peter Murcock.* New York: McGraw-Hill.

————. 1984. *The Shoshoni-Crow Sun Dance.* Norman: University of Oklahoma Press.

Watembach, Karen. 1983. History of the Catechesis of the Catholic Church on the Crow Reservation. Master's thesis, Montana State University, Bozeman.

Wildschut, William, and John Ewers. 1959. *Crow Indian Beadwork: A Descriptive and Historical Study.* New York: Museum of the American Indian.

————. 1975. *Crow Indian Medicine Bundles.* 2d ed. New York: Museum of the American Indian.

Yellowtail, Robert, Sr. 1973. *At Crow Fair.* Albuquerque, New Mexico: Wowapi.

## Other Materials

Benedict, Ruth. 1923. *The Concept of the Guardian Spirit in North America.* Memoir 29. American Anthropological Association, Lancaster, Pa.

Brown, Joseph, ed. 1953. *The Sacred Pipe: Black Elk's Account of the Seven Rites of the Oglala Sioux.* Norman: University of Oklahoma Press.

Eliade, Mircea. 1954. *Myth of the Eternal Return, or Cosmos and History.* Princeton, N.J.: Princeton University Press.

Ewers, John C. 1955. *The Horse in Blackfoot Indian Culture, with Comparative Material from Other Western Tribes.* Washington, D.C: Smithsonian Institution Press.

Geertz, Clifford. 1973. *The Interpretation of Cultures.* New York: Basic Books.

Gill, Sam D. 1977. Prayer as Person: The Performative Force in Navajo Prayer Acts. *History of Religions* 17:143–57.

Hall, Robert. 1985. Medicine Wheels, Sun Circles, and the

Magic of World Center Shrines. *Plains Anthropologist* 30: 181–93.

Hultkrantz, Åke. 1976. The Contribution of the Study of North American Indian Religions to the History of Religions. In Walter H. Capps, ed. *Seeing with the Native Eye: Contributions to the Study of Native American Religion* New York: Harper & Row.

Kearney, Michael. 1975. World View Theory and Study. In *Annual Review of Anthropology* 4:247–70. Palo Alto, Calif.: Annual Review, Inc.

LaBarre, Western. 1969. *The Peyote Cult.* New York: Schocken Books.

Momaday, N. Scott. 1983. The Man Made of Words. In Sam Gill. *Native American Traditions: Sources and Interpretations.* Belmont, Calif.: Wadsworth Publishing. Originally published in 1970.

Ortiz, Alfonso. 1969. *The Tewa World: Space, Time, Being, and Becoming in a Pueblo Society.* Chicago: University of Chicago Press.

Plato. 1968. *The Republic.* Trans. by B. Jowett. New York: Airmont.

Walker, J. R. 1917. The Sun Dance and Other Ceremonies of the Oglala Division of the Teton Dakota. *Anthropological Papers of the American Museum of Natural History,* 16:51–221. Reprint, New York: AMS Reprint.

# Index